JUPITER LAUGHS

JUPITER LAUGHS

A Play in Three Acts

by

A. J. CRONIN

LONDON
VICTOR GOLLANCZ LTD
1941

822
CRO

PRINTED IN GREAT BRITAIN BY RICHARD CLAY AND COMPANY, LTD. (T.U.),
BUNGAY, SUFFOLK.

CHARACTERS

EDGAR BRAGG, Medical Superintendent of Hopewell Towers

GLADYS BRAGG, his wife

PAUL VENNER

RICHARD DREWETT

GEORGE THOROGOOD

MARY MURRAY

} Assistant Physicians at Hopewell Towers

FANNY LEEMING, Matron at Hopewell Towers

JENNIE, a Maid at Hopewell Towers

ALBERT CHIVERS, District Representative of Glyster's

MARTHA FOSTER, Wife of a patient at Hopewell Towers

SYNOPSIS OF SCENES

ACT I

SCENE I. The doctors' common-room at Hopewell Towers. A winter afternoon.

SCENE II. The Same. Sunday morning, six weeks later. (The Curtain will be lowered during this scene to denote the passage of about eight hours.)

ACT II

SCENE I. The Same. A spring afternoon, one month later.

SCENE II. The Same. Evening, two days later.

ACT III

The Same. Forenoon, one month later.

ACT I

SCENE I

SCENE: *The doctors' common-room at Hopewell Towers.*

TIME: *Towards half-past three of a wet winter afternoon.*

It is a biggish room, much lived in, a combination of dining- and sitting-room, with sideboard Left, dining-table Centre, alcove with gramophone, small table and window at Back. To Right of this a worn leather couch, cottage piano, two leather armchairs, indian clubs, letter-rack, pegs with white coats. The fireplace is in the Right wall. There are three doors. Back Centre is the main door, opening to outer passage. In the Left wall a door gives access to domestic and doctors' quarters. In the Right wall (forward) another door of significance to the play.

DR. DREWETT, *an old man, possibly over seventy, lean, stooping, dry, with a calm, clean-shaven, intellectual face and an air of cynical detachment, is playing patience in the alcove.*

DR. THOROGOOD, *twenty-six, heavy, athletic, very correct, with briar pipe and public-school tie, in clean white short clinical jacket, is standing at the small table forward mixing a glass winchester of Dakin's solution.*

THOROGOOD (*pausing*)

I'm worried.

DREWETT

Dear me.

9

THOROGOOD (*frowning*)

About Foster! (*He goes to the gramophone and puts on a popular musical-comedy number.*)

DREWETT (*wincing*)

Does that allay your anxiety?

THOROGOOD

Lovely tune.   (*Pauses.*)   The Chief ought to take action.

DREWETT

I shouldn't (*plays card*) if I were you (*plays another*)—why do they put no red nines in the packs nowadays?—encourage your dear uncle to interfere with Venner and his patients.

THOROGOOD (*irritably*)

Drewett, don't harp on Dr. Bragg being my uncle. I'm here like the rest of you—pulling my weight—and I do bar the way Venner's handling this case.

DREWETT

Occasionally, Thorogood (*playing card*), I wish you didn't know everything.

THOROGOOD (*complacently*)

I know my job.   And I get on with it.

DR. VENNER ENTERS abruptly *Back Centre, carrying dripping old umbrella.   PAUL VENNER is about twenty-eight years of age, spare, dark, intense, with a slightly dissolute air, carelessly dressed in tweed jacket and grey flannel trousers.   All his movements are overstrung, charged with a restless, defiant, bitter*

10

energy. At present he looks tired and badly needs a shave. He slings umbrella on the table beside Dr. Thorogood.

VENNER

Present from Munich. I thought I asked you by special request not to play that masterpiece.

THOROGOOD

We've got to play something to drown the shindy your prize patient's been kicking up all afternoon.

VENNER

Then play music!

THOROGOOD

One of your lamented father's compositions?

VENNER

My father was a rotten composer. But he knew what it was all about, poor devil! (*He lifts moving record off the gramophone.*) Put this on again and I'll liquidate it on your permanent wave.

THOROGOOD

You try! And don't forget I boxed for Giggleswick— while you were continental pub-crawling!

VENNER (*flinging his hat at peg*)
They didn't teach you *la savate*—from behind!

THOROGOOD (*indignant*)
I'd hope not! (*Pugnacious*) Why don't you give Foster an injection? Quieten the blighter down?

VENNER

George, you're so stupid that even I can't help noticing it sometimes. (*Going to sideboard and lifting the cover from the hotplate, his expression disgusted.*) Is this my lunch?

THOROGOOD (*grins*)

It was!

VENNER (*going to door L.*)

Jennie! Jennie! (*There is no answer. Louder.*) Jennie! *He swings round and presses the bell by the mantelpiece.*

MATRON LEEMING ENTERS L. *She is a pale, contained woman of forty-five with an erect figure and a cold, secretive, proper face. There is about her something striving, tortured and insidious. She faces Venner with suppressed resentment.*

MATRON

Haven't I asked you, Dr. Venner, not to shout for the maid? I've trouble enough with my domestic staff. Jennie is busy, preparing the new doctor's room.   What do you want?

VENNER

Something to eat.

MATRON

You lunch is on the hotplate.

VENNER

Hotplate! It's a crematorium!

MATRON

I'm not responsible if you disregard the proper meal-

12

times and waste hours of your time in there. (*She gives an utterly vindictive nod towards the closed door R.*)

VENNER (*contemplating her*)

Dear Fanny! My little desert flower!

MATRON (*rising voice*)

I asked you not to refer to me by my Christian name, Dr. Venner. You give me my place and I'll give you yours.

VENNER (*with a burst of bitter laughter*)

Give you your place! Don't you take it! You worm yourself in everywhere. You preside at our meals when we don't want you. Because your virginal bedchamber's in this block you come butting in here every minute of the dav. Besides taking every chance to run with tales to Bra ,g, to extend your influence and authority.

MATRON (*breathing quickly*)

Be careful, Dr. Venner, with your insolence. I only use this common-room because I'm forced to, because I haven't got a sitting-room of my own. Every other matron in an institution like this has a room of her own. Why shouldn't I have one? (*Loud voice*) I ought to have that room in there (*again indicates the door R.*) that's wasted and thrown away on your highflown experiments.

VENNER

I had that room for a lab. before your friend Bragg bought this knacker's yard. And I mean to keep it.

13

MATRON

Time will tell, Dr. Venner. I haven't given years of my life to Hopewell Towers for nothing. And I will say this. If I was to inform Dr. Bragg of certain things within my knowledge, I swear you'd have your notice.

VENNER

My notice! (*Laughs shortly.*) The idiom of the kitchen still sticks to you, Fanny!

MATRON (*now seething with rage, gives him a malignant look but controls herself with a great effort*)

I won't prolong this discussion, Dr. Venner.

VENNER

Thank God for small mercies!

EXIT MATRON *L.*

DREWETT

Was that wise, Venner?

VENNER

What? Oh, surely it's common knowledge—she started her career twenty years ago as a maid in Blackton Home before she had the luck to step into a probationer's job?

DREWETT

She won't forgive you for reminding her.

VENNER (*moodily*)

Damn her forgiveness! I'm hungry. She'll hold back our tea out of spite.

14

DREWETT

On the contrary, we shall have it the moment the new doctor arrives. Our peculiar matron delights in creating good impressions—an expression of her libido!

VENNER (*lights a cigarette and flings himself into a chair*)
When is this confounded woman coming?

DREWETT

She was due at Parchester by the three o'clock train. As the Chief and his missis were driving in, shopping, they said they'd fetch her out.

VENNER

Charming. The thought of a woman doctor in this place . . .

DREWETT (*cynically*)
An idyll?

VENNER

An emetic!

THOROGOOD

She's only temporary—while Sargent's away—and there's no reason why a good sensible middle-aged woman shouldn't fit into the scheme of things.

DREWETT (*absently*)
I believe she comes from Scotland.

VENNER

Scrawny and sandy. (*Imitating Scots accent*) Do ye poultice yer pneumonias, doctor? I know the type.

DREWETT (*dryly*)

Not yours, I imagine.

THOROGOOD (*corks the winchester, now filled with milky solution*)

That's a good job done!

VENNER

Nunkey's a little scientist!

THOROGOOD

Someone's got to be decent enough to do the dispensing. What happened to those three litres of ether that came in from Glyster's the other day?

VENNER

Ah! My sin has found me out!

THOROGOOD

I thought you'd taken them for your confounded experiments! (*He lifts winchester and goes to door.*) You've got a nerve!

VENNER (*laughs*)

I've got the ether!

EXIT THOROGOOD *Back Centre.*

DREWETT (*incidentally*)

How is Foster today?

VENNER

Physically unchanged—you know his heart's rotten. Mentally there's a marvellous reaction to the increased dosage—checked on the eosinophilia-control. (*He unconsciously sits up, his whole bearing altered, his expression animated, intense.*) As a matter of fact, Drewett—this last modification of my formula—God! it's really exciting me. By altering the proportion of di-sodium phosphate, previously ·01, in ten per cent sterile solution, I double the strength and purity of my original betrazol.

Sound of a car outside.

DREWETT

Not that I care tuppence . . . (*detached*). You really think you can cure Foster?

VENNER (*intently*)

Drewett, I swear I can! But it isn't a question of individual cases! If my calculations are correct, if I've really got it! . . . (*He jumps up excitedly, pulls a key from his pocket and advances to open the door R.*) Wait! I'll show you!

ENTER THOROGOOD, *wiping his hands on small towel.*

THOROGOOD

They're here.

VENNER *stops, lets the key slip back into his pocket. He stands, arrested, at the door R.* THOROGOOD *adjusts his tie, quickly smooths his hair with pocket comb.*

DR. BRAGG ENTERS *Back Centre, followed by* DR. MARY MURRAY. EDGAR BRAGG *is a successful pompous man of about fifty. He is dressed in a highly professional style: cutaway coat, striped trousers, winged collar, and shows a good deal of stiff white cuff.*

Behind him, MARY MURRAY *is the complete antithesis of the expected type. She is only twenty-two, and most unusually pretty. Her expression has a sweet and spiritual loveliness. She wears a costume of neat blue serge.*

BRAGG (*advancing with bounding assurance*)

Good afternoon, gentlemen. (*Turning, wave of hand*) Your future colleagues, Dr. Murray. On my right, Dr. Drewett, an old and trusted member of the staff, ripe in years, perhaps, but ripe also in discretion and experience.

MARY

How do you do?

DREWETT *bows.*

BRAGG

On my left, my nephew, Dr. Thorogood—leader of our football eleven, conductor of our choral society, a stout upholder, like myself, of the wise adage, mens sana in corpore sano. A fine fellow!

THOROGOOD (*heartily shaking hands*)

Pleased to meet you.

BRAGG

And (*deprecating gesture*) Dr. Venner.

MARY

How do you do?

The MATRON ENTERS *unobtrusively L., followed by* JENNIE, *who begins to set the tea.*

BRAGG

Ah! You always appear precisely when you are wanted!

18

Dr. Murray—Miss Leeming, our most worthy matron. I vouch for her (*platform attitude*), the most capable in England!

MATRON (*advancing, his devoted slave*)
You're too kind, Dr. Bragg. (*She shakes hands with Mary.*) It's an honour to work at Hopewell Towers.

BRAGG
Yes, Dr. Murray. Not only are we the most select private nerve clinic in the county, but, thanks to our affiliation with the Parchester Board—on which as J.P. I occupy the chair—we admit a limited number of the working class—opening our doors to all nervous disorders, also for those who are—ahem!—mentally afflicted. We have vegetables from our own gardens, produce from the home farm, an artesian well penetrating eight hundred feet to the millstone grits! Now—report to me in my office at five sharp. Matron will show you to your room.

MARY
Thank you. I'd like to wash before tea.

MARY *prepares to leave the room. Confused by her new surroundings, she makes to exit by door R. at which* VENNER *stands, his face still contorted by Bragg's peroration.*

VENNER (*with offensive politeness*)
Not that way.

MARY (*startled*)
I'm sorry.

She turns, follows MATRON. THEY EXIT L. *The table is now laid for tea.* JENNIE EXIT L.

19

BRAGG (*formally to* DREWETT *and* THOROGOOD *at back of room*)

Excuse us, gentlemen.

He takes Venner aside while DREWETT *glances at patience cards, and* THOROGOOD, *pretending to clean pipe, listens.*

Dr. Venner, have you written up those case-books?

VENNER

Not yet.

BRAGG

Why not?

VENNER

Haven't had time.

BRAGG (*his temper rising*)

You must find time, Dr. Venner. I will not have the routine of my institution upset by your slipshod opportunism. Why haven't you shaved today?

VENNER

Some days I don't trust myself with a razor.

BRAGG (*sneeringly facetious*)

Afraid you might cut your throat, eh?

VENNER

No, yours.

BRAGG

That's enough, Dr. Venner. I must request you, once again, to dress, and generally comport yourself, in a manner befitting my establishment.

VENNER (*mockingly*)

What's the betting I cure more patients in my shirt-sleeves in six months than you do in a cutaway coat in six years?

BRAGG (*frigidly*)

I do not bet, Dr. Venner. But I do know that your special patient, Foster, has been most troublesome this week.

VENNER

I expect him to be troublesome.

BRAGG

He should have a sedative.

VENNER (*flashing out*)

I won't dope him into insensibility. Start that and he's done for. (*Quietly*) So long as I'm running your psychiatric ward, Dr. Bragg—I'm running it scientifically.

The door Back Centre opens and GLADYS BRAGG ENTERS. *She is about thirty-four, an attractive, rather fastidious woman, tastefully dressed, playfully sophisticated on the surface but with something underneath.*

GLADYS

Goodness! Have I disturbed a session of the mortuary committee?

BRAGG (*his expression relaxing at the sight of* GLADYS, *he beams at her with uxorious fondness*)

Quite all right, my dear. I've said all I had to say.

21

GLADYS (*smiling at* VENNER)

The minute I put the car away I flew round with your cigarettes. A hundred, wasn't it?

VENNER

Yes. (*He accepts the packet mechanically.*) Thank you, Mrs. Bragg.

GLADYS

Well! I like that! What about my commission?

VENNER

Oh! (*He opens the box and offers her a cigarette.*)

GLADYS

Thank you.

BRAGG (*quickly and fondly proffers a light*)

Are you sure you're not smoking too much, G.?

GLADYS

What a question—before Dr. Venner—with his fifty a day. I'm sure he has smoker's heart.

BRAGG (*pettishly*)

I'm not concerned with the state of Dr. Venner's heart, Gladys. Really, we must be going, my dear. I've got Glyster's man waiting on me.

GLADYS (*gaily, prolonging her stay*)

You're always rushing me off, Edgar. I want the verdict on the new locum. (*Wrinkling up her nose.*) Isn't she a little—ethereal—what d'you think, George?

22

THOROGOOD (*critically*)

Too young.

DREWETT (*dryly*)

You can't expect me to run her down, Mrs. Bragg.
I've only just met her.

VENNER *laughs.* JENNIE ENTERS R. *bringing in a large
pot of tea.*

BRAGG

Come, my dear. (*He takes Gladys' arm with possessive
fondness.*) You're such a little chatterbox once you
start!

EXIT BRAGG *and* GLADYS *Back Centre.* JENNIE *sounds
the small gong on the sideboard.*

MATRON *and* MARY ENTER L. *They* ALL *sit down to
tea,* MATRON *presiding.*

MATRON

Sugar, Dr. Murray?

MARY

Two lumps, please.

VENNER (*urbanely*)

Seasonable weather for January?

MARY (*smile*)

Rain is always seasonable in Scotland.

THOROGOOD (*obviously attracted*)

Jolly good for the complexion, anyhow. (*Admiring
look.*) Hope you didn't have a trying journey?

MARY (*cheerfully*)

It wasn't too bad.

VENNER

Your people all well?

MARY

I have no people.

VENNER (*sad voice*)

Pity! I too am an orphan.

THOROGOOD

Take no notice of him, Dr. Murray.

DREWETT (*hitherto old man's absorption with his food*)

Nor of him! Although he's Dr. Bragg's nephew and the son of a rich mineral-water manufacturer in Sutton Coldfield he's already got a fiancee! She writes to him every day.

VENNER *laughs.*

THOROGOOD (*huffily*)

None of your business!

VENNER

What providential planet brought you to Hopewell Towers, doctor? Perhaps you were attracted by the fame of our proprietor, Dr. Edgar Bragg?

MARY

No, I hadn't heard of him.

VENNER

Impossible! Good God! Drewett, such is the reward

of the man who introduced home-grown brussel sprouts in the treatment of disseminated sclerosis.

MATRON

Some more toast, Dr. Murray?

VENNER (*effusively, not to be diverted*)

Yes, do, doctor! Or some of our millstone grits plumcake! We must keep our strength up. Eh, Matron? Mens sana in corporis sanitas, meaning, though I need not translate, " eat when you can, for you damned well can't when you want to ". But why *have* you come here?

MARY (*openly, sincerely*)

It's quite simple. I'm not specially interested in this work. My heart and soul are bound up in a very different cause. I am going to be a missionary, a medical missionary.

VENNER (*stupefied*)

What!

MARY (*simply, unshaken*)

Yes, I'm going out to Shantchen, in China. My father was a missionary there; he worked and died there. So did my mother. I graduated only last month. Dr. King isn't quite ready for me at our mission hospital. And besides . . . (*she smiles faintly*) I wanted to earn enough to pay my fare. I was fortunate to see this advertisement in the ' Lancet '. And here I am.

VENNER

Good God! (*Pause.*) So that's it.

MARY

Yes.

VENNER (*smoothly*)

Naturally you speak Chinese?

MARY

A little. When I was a child I learned a good many words—and I've been studying hard. . . .

VENNER

Splendid, splendid! It will be a great joy to converse with you. Tell me, doctor—chu-chow chin chin chung lung soo?

DREWETT (*quietly*)

Don't go too far, Venner.

VENNER (*pidgin English*)

Allee nicee people listen velly close. I givee one piece Sermon to lee Heathen. Oh, my yellow blethren, I come here teach you follee of you ways. Allee same delusion andee snare. This I ploove to you allee same mist alba thlee times day. Come to surgely door, please. We now sing one piece hymn: " Oh, God, makee help in ages past."

MATRON (*interposing heatedly*)

Really, Dr. Venner, you should be ashamed of yourself.

THOROGOOD

I've a good mind to sock you on the jaw.

VENNER

Not before the ladies, George.

26

MARY

I don't mind for myself. But my work! Dr. Venner, your idea of a missionary seems to come from an out-of-date comic strip. There happens to be a war in China with millions of homeless—starvation—air raids—cholera. Women and little children undergoing unbelievable suffering—crying out for bread——

VENNER

Why wrap your loaf up in a text?

MARY

Only to show them that it comes from God!

VENNER

Like the bombs.

MARY

These come from men who have forgotten God!

VENNER

Then why not fling your tracts at the dictators?

MARY

As if they mattered! (*Carried away*) They'd cease to exist if only all the peoples of the earth believed in God —obeyed His laws—remembered how and why He created us!

VENNER (*laughs*)

And that, dear children, ends our bedtime story for this evening. Tomorrow you shall hear what the naughty serpent did to Auntie Evie.

ENTER ALBERT CHIVERS *Back Centre.* *He looks exactly what he is, a prosperous commercial traveller, but although he wears brown shoes with a blue suit he has a shrewd eye in his shining face.*

CHIVERS

Evening, all. I hope I don't intrude.

DREWETT

Fortunately you do. Dr. Murray, allow me to present Mr. Chivers, District Representative of Glyster's.

CHIVERS (*beaming*)

The finest drug house without exception in the kingdom. Pleased to meet you, miss—doctor, I should say. Biggest regret of my life that I wasn't brought out for a doctor myself. I'll see that my youngster goes through, though. I love the profession. He's only seven, mind you. But what a lad!

VENNER

You look happy, Chivers. Just been saved?

CHIVERS

Not a word! (*He winks.*) Promotion! Our Mr. Glyster is talking about moving me to London—general sales manager. Sunday last I said to the wife, Blodwen, I said—she's a Welshwoman, Dr. Murray: I married her in Swansea: had our honeymoon at the Mumbles, we didn't mind the rain—Blodwen, I said, if I watch my p's and q's—I was overhauling the lawnmower at the time—I doubt, I said, come the spring, if I shall cut that lawn again!

VENNER

Congratulations! If you've any weed-killer left over let me have it for Bragg!

CHIVERS

Ha! Ha! You don't mean that, Dr. Venner—no, doctor, not you! Matter of fact, I've just had my order (*Taps bulging pocket.*) . . . You're the very man I came to see! Dr. Venner, have you thought over Mr. Glyster's offer?

DREWETT

What's this?

CHIVERS

£500 a year's not to be sneezed at, Dr. Venner. Plus the distinction of being one of the picked staff of twenty assistant research physicians to the House of Glyster.

VENNER *exchanges a look with* DREWETT; BOTH *laugh.*

VENNER

I'm sorry, Mr. Chivers. I appreciate the compliment. But, as I told you, there is absolutely nothing doing.

CHIVERS (*looking from one to the other*)

Well! I'm not beat yet, doctor. Maybe we can raise the guv'nor an extra fifty quid between us. Always buys a few Coronas, eh? Ha! Ha! How's the work proceeding?

VENNER

What work?

CHIVERS (*laughing heartily*)

What work! Aha! That's good. But you can't kid

me, sir. I can smell a new line a mile away. Only last night, as I was dropping off, I sat up in bed and said to the wife, Blod, I said, that fellow Venner—pardon the familiarity, doctor—he's got something! Yes, indeed, that's the very words I uttered. Well! Keep the proposition before you, Dr. Venner. I'll have to be getting along.

THOROGOOD (*rising*)

You might look into the dispensary with me on your way out. I think we're short of tinct. camph co.

CHIVERS

I'm with you, doctor. Never refuse an order or a pal is the motto of yours truly, Albert Chivers. All the best, Dr. Venner. Evening, all.

EXEUNT THOROGOOD *and* CHIVERS *Back Centre.*

VENNER

Excuse me, I want to look at a test. (*Goes to door R., extinguishes his cigarette, uses key.*)

EXIT VENNER.

MATRON (*staring at closed door R.*)

I'm sure we were all sorry for such an exhibition on Dr. Venner's part, Dr. Murray, but it had to come sooner or later. I hope I'm not exceeding my position when I say he's impossible. (*Poison in her voice*) Everybody in Hopewell Towers detests him.

DREWETT

Everybody, Matron?

MATRON

Your devotion to him is absurd, Dr. Drewett.

DREWETT

I? I'm devoted to no one—but myself.

MATRON (*rising crossly*)

It's my evening for duty in the hall. I must get my knitting.

EXIT MATRON *L.*

DREWETT (*turning to Mary*)

My dear young woman, Venner's conduct *was* unpardonable. Oh! I'm not excusing him. I—I've no interest in the wretched fellow. But—well—life hasn't been exactly easy for him. His childhood . . .

MARY

Was it unhappy?

DREWETT (*dryly*)

Shall we say eventful! His father—sensitive, useless, good family—set out to be another Mozart and died scraping a fiddle in a café in Ostende. His mother—he showed me her photograph once—she must have been absurdly beautiful (*cynically*) before she'd danced to the fiddler's tune. Well, she struggled on—until she couldn't any longer. Life—and death—can be so disgustingly melodramatic. (*Pause.*) Paul, aged ten, was pulled half dead out of the gas-filled lodging.

MARY (*moved*)

Oh, poor boy!

DREWETT

Ah, that was only the beginning. Afterwards his education was thrown to him by his grandfather—like scraps of dry biscuit to a stray dog. Amusing—but not for the dog!

MARY (*slowly*)

I'm not surprised he's bitter. (*Quickly*) But he's clever, isn't he?

DREWETT

I believe the cliché is—genius. You don't know his work with Von Reiter at the Budapest Imperial Hospital —beta-methylenetetrazol, intravenously, in the treatment of schizophrenia? (*She shakes her head.*) I thought not. That, of course, is the real explanation of Venner's bitterness.

MARY

Tell me?

DREWETT (*indifferently*)

Oh, he was working with—or rather under—Reiter, and obtaining encouraging results. But the shock reactions on the patient were so severe the treatment seemed useless. (*Breaks off.*) I'm boring you—in fact, I'm boring myself.

MARY

Oh, no; please go on.

DREWETT

Well—Reiter's hypothesis was that shock was essential in the therapy. Venner, on the contrary, believed the improvement due to specific stimulation of the functionally inactive cerebral cells, by some element in an otherwise deleterious drug. And he said so! There was a frightful row. It came to such a point the civil authorities were called in. Venner was kicked out of the country minus his papers, his apparatus, and the results of all his experiments.

MARY (*slowly*)

That was enough to break any man's heart.

DREWETT

It only hardened Venner's. He came home—took this rotten crib because it offered him control of a psychiatric ward, set to work to justify himself. Now, after four years, he's produced a substance, betrazol, which—he says—stimulates without shock, specifically regenerates nerve-cells. Unless my wits are completely senile, he's on the threshold of a discovery which will revolutionise our whole conception of the treatment of nervous disorders. (*Suddenly*) Now . . . you won't let him upset you.

MARY

I'm not so easily upset. (*Slowly*) I'm glad you told me. There's something in his face which makes me sorry for him.

Buzzer goes outside.

DREWETT (*rising*)

I must show you the office. (*He grimaces at Mary.*) That nuisance means evening rounds.

MARY *and* DREWETT GO OUT *Back Centre.*

VENNER ENTERS R., *carrying small flask holding yellow crystals, stoppered with cottonwool. At the same time* MATRON ENTERS L., *a bag on her arm from which a hank of wool trails.*

VENNER (*in passing*)

Evening, Fanny. Taking out the dog?

EXIT MATRON *Back Centre.*

VENNER, *in no hurry to answer the buzzer, sets flask on table, lights a cigarette, goes to the gramophone and puts on a record. It is Chopin's B flat minor Sonata, Opus 35. He is listening to it with a remote intentness when* GLADYS BRAGG ENTERS *Back Centre.*

GLADYS

Hello! Hard at work?

VENNER (*listening*)

Ssh!

GLADYS

Why must you always play that record?

VENNER

It helps me to forget the futile tragedy of existence. And I damn well can't play it well enough myself!

GLADYS

It is nice—but I want to talk. (*Switching off the gramophone.*) When I came in with Edgar I forgot to give you your change. (*Advances towards him, smiling.*) And this. (*Puts her arms round him and kisses him with abandon.*) I've

34

hardly *seen* you these last few days. You still love me, don't you, darling?

GLADYS (*reproachfully, real feeling*)

VENNER (*not unkindly*)

Did I ever say I loved you?

GLADYS (*reproachfully, real feeling*)

Paul! After all our wonderful times together. (*Sudden gravity*) I don't know how I'd stand this place without you.

VENNER

You've got Edgar.

GLADYS

Oh, Edgar! (*Lightly*) He's so full of the conference next month—dreams he's been made President of the Psychological Association! (*Pause.*) Why *did* I marry him, Paul?

VENNER

Didn't you guess you'd have to sleep with him?

GLADYS (*frowning slightly*)

He's so dull. But, then (*rueful smile*), my youth was an essay in the commonplace.

VENNER

Was it?

GLADYS

Our house in Queen's Gate was always full of the most crashing bores—especially after father took silk. And mother—through her brother being a canon at Westminster—knew (*smile*) such nice stupid people.

35

VENNER

Stop pretending not to be a snob, Gladys.

GLADYS (*shaking her head, still faintly ironic smile*)

That's the last thing I am! But—well—on the fringes of Knightsbridge—one recognises blue blood!

VENNER

You mean Kensington Gore!

GLADYS (*laughs*)

Exactly! Still (*dreamily*) I do think of London such a lot—the shops—the buses running along Piccadilly—the theatres. I often wish we could do a first night together. I'd wear my nice gold lame frock. . . .

VENNER

The one you seduced me in.

GLADYS

Darling, must you call everything by its improper name? I meant my newest rag, high in the waist, with a tight bodice and pleated skirt. We'd dine beforehand at Henri's—you know?

VENNER

Menu in French, cooking in English.

GLADYS (*pouting*)

I won't go on. (*Stroking his head.*) How absurdly thick your hair is! Edgar's restorers are an awful swindle. (*Tenderly*) Paul, do let's meet tonight.

36

VENNER

I'm afraid I'm busy.

GLADYS

But—darling!

VENNER (*exasperated*)

Please don't slop. (*Sudden resolve*) Gladys! Don't you think——

GLADYS (*quickly*)

It isn't as if we were doing anything frightfully wrong (*wry smile*)—so long as Edgar doesn't find out!

VENNER (*ironical again*)

I see your point of view.

GLADYS (*half mocking, half tender*)

I'm not an abandoned woman, Paul,—merely a horribly fed-up one. I remember my reverend uncle once said——

VENNER (*impatiently*)

Oh, Gladys, stop chasing your reputation in the canon's mouth!

GLADYS (*drawn up short—hurt and suddenly serious*)

Must we go on being clever with one another? You know, my dear—I'm most terribly fond of you.

VENNER

Isn't it rather a mistake—to tell me?

37

GLADYS

Not very subtle, perhaps—but for once most terribly
true. These last six months you've made me so happy.
You've changed the utter boredom of this ghastly place.
And all because—there have been moments—when you've
said you cared.

VENNER (*quickly*)

There are moments when any man tells any woman
he adores her.

GLADYS

They're not less sweet for that! (*Softly*) Don't let's
argue, Paul! You will come tonight, won't you?

VENNER (*hesitates, then without enthusiasm*)

Oh, all right.

GLADYS

The usual place. Behind the chapel.

She is about to kiss him when MATRON ENTERS *Back Centre,
wearing her cape. Hastily* GLADYS *breaks away.* VENNER
picks up flask of crystals from table.

Oh, Matron, it's you! Dr. Venner was just showing
me his new preparation. I'm so interested—what d'you
call it, doctor?

VENNER (*shortly*)

Betrazol.

GLADYS

Of course! Charming colour, isn't it, Matron?

MATRON (*immobile, comprehending*)

Very charming, Mrs. Bragg.

MATRON *goes to alcove, takes up half-knitted sock.*

VENNER

Ah, you forgot the sock, Matron. Another pair for Dr. Bragg?

MATRON (*defiantly*)

Yes, they are for Dr. Bragg; he appreciates them. And I knit them open and proper.

VENNER (*faint smile*)

With pure wool—eh, Matron? (*Lifts flask of crystals.* GOES OUT *Back Centre.*)

MATRON (*false smile*)

Smart, isn't he?

GLADYS

I prefer him when he's serious.

MATRON

I don't really hold it against him. Not me. It's what he's come through makes him so nervy—all that work he did abroad—lost so sudden and unexpected. It quite worries me sometimes.

GLADYS

Why? He's done it again.

39

MATRON

That's what I mean. I can't help thinking, if the same thing should happen—it makes me shiver. (*Pauses.*) Dr. Venner's so careless himself—or suppose somebody, say Jennie, should drop a match——

GLADYS

Nonsense! He keeps his laboratory safely locked.

MATRON

Yes, he has the key. But still—why, he'd go crazy.

GLADYS

You're morbid, Matron. (*Moving to door*) I'm going before I catch the germ. Good night.

MATRON

Good night, Mrs. Bragg.

EXIT GLADYS *Back Centre.*

MATRON *stands, then slowly goes to door of laboratory, leans against it and softly turns the handle.*

JENNIE ENTERS *suddenly with tray.*

MATRON (*turning furiously*)

Why don't you knock when you come in? Sneaking up behind me like that!

JENNIE

I wasn't, Matron. I—I only came to clear——

40

Don't answer me back.   Keep your place—and give me mine!

Exit Matron *Back Centre.*

CURTAIN

ACT I

SCENE: *The doctors' common-room.*

TIME: *Quarter to eleven on Sunday morning, six weeks later.*
The church bells of Hopewell Towers Chapel are beginning.
They sound regularly, softly. The room looks spruce and
clean, wearing a Sabbath polish.

> *Standing waiting, gloved, dressed in cap and outdoor*
> *uniform, is* MATRON. *Her erect, attentive figure is*
> *solitary in the room. But immediately* DR. BRAGG
> ENTERS *Back Centre and bustles into his room. He is*
> *dressed immaculately, wears a top hat and spats.*

BRAGG (*in great spirits*)

Ah! You're ready, Matron. A lovely morning. Mrs.
Bragg is getting out the car.

MATRON

I'm highly honoured, Dr. Bragg. You know—(*eyes
downcast*)—I once held a very humble position at
Blackton.

BRAGG (*nods, approving her humility*)

Today the feather is in your cap, Matron—Hopewell,
not Blackton, is the venue of next month's conference!

MATRON

I believe they're sick with jealousy. (*Pause.*) Wouldn't it be wonderful if they elected you the new President, Dr. Bragg?

BRAGG

I! Pooh, my dear Matron. Mind you, if they *did*, I flatter myself I wouldn't let them down!

MATRON (*tortured, yearning*)

Your career means everything to me, Dr. Bragg. Some women might laugh and treat it lightly—but to me it's the most important thing in the world!

BRAGG (*moving R.*)

Thank you.

MATRON

Dr. Bragg!

BRAGG (*stops*)

Yes?

MATRON (*showing scarf which she has held behind her back*)

This scarf was found in the grounds this morning.

BRAGG

Why—it's my wife's!

MATRON

Oh—really?

BRAGG

She must have dropped it.

43

MATRON (*steps forward*)

Surely not! It was found in the little shrubbery behind the chapel.

BRAGG (*obtuse*)

In the shrubbery?

MATRON

Right amongst the bushes. (*Little laugh.*) Isn't it odd?

BRAGG

The wind must have taken it.

MATRON (*another step nearer*)

But—there wasn't any wind last night, Dr. Bragg.

BRAGG

What nonsense are you talking?

MATRON (*pressing her face against scarf*)

It does smell—inviting!

BRAGG (*brusquely*)

Please! (*He snatches scarf from her with pompous resentment.*) I don't like my wife's things pawed by the entire nursing staff!

MATRON (*repulsed Matron shivers, stands trembling, abashed. Then she forces a pale smile*)

I'm sure I beg your pardon, Dr. Bragg. It's you I think of—first and last.

Enter Mary *and* Thorogood *at Left. Both are dressed for church.* Mary *carries some hymn-books.*

THOROGOOD

Morning, sir.

BRAGG

Good morning, George. Morning, Dr. Murray. (*Approvingly*) On your way to church? (*Glancing at his watch*) Where's Venner?

THOROGOOD

He wasn't down to breakfast.

BRAGG

What! Not up yet!

MARY (*quickly*)

Oh, yes, he's up. At least . . .

MATRON

Jennie tells me his bed wasn't slept in last night.

BRAGG (*thundering*)

Has he been out of the institution?

MARY

Oh, no, Dr. Bragg. I think he's been up all night—working in his laboratory.

MATRON (*icily*)

It's my belief he's in there now.

They all look at door R.

BRAGG

Up all night! I never heard of anything so irregular in all my life. Call him, Matron!

MATRON (*advancing and knocking at door R.*)

Dr. Venner! (*There is no answer. Knocking louder*) Dr. Venner! Dr. Venner! The Chief wishes to speak to you.

A moment's pause, then the door R. opens and VENNER ENTERS, *yawning, hair tousled, collar undone, holding a sheaf of papers in his hand. He wears an old stained lab. coat, is tired and dejected. He gazes rather dizzily at the well-dressed little group centred round Bragg.*

VENNER

Morning, everybody. All on your way to washup. Why, no, I forgot. (*Looking at Bragg*) You and Fanny are off joy-riding today.

BRAGG

The Matron and myself are making an official visit to our friends and colleagues at Blackton Home. My wife is driving us over.

VENNER (*yawning again*)

She'll enjoy that. (*Moving in a fatigued manner to side-board, lifts cover of hotplate.*) Of course not. Not a cross section of infected bacon, not a charred remnant of cirrhotic kidney. (*He pours himself out a glass of whisky and soda.*)

46

BRAGG (*scarcely able to restrain himself*)

I must say, Dr. Venner, you show a shining example. Whisky! And on a Sunday morning!

VENNER

Your logic should get you into Parliament. (*With dark sullenness*) I've been working twelve hours on a stretch. I need a stimulant. What difference whether I take it on Sunday morning or Saturday night?

BRAGG

Very little, I imagine, to a man who turns night into day. (*With an air of purpose he straightens the pile of books on the small table in front of him.*)

MARY (*nervously, with a glance at Bragg*)

You'll excuse us, Dr. Bragg.

BRAGG (*arresting her with a gesture*)

Stay! Both of you! What I have to say is best said publicly. Dr. Venner, you observe these case-books upon that table?

VENNER

Mistily, Edgar.

BRAGG

For the second time in four months they have fallen six weeks in arrears. While I may tolerate your unorthodox methods of treatment, this strikes at the very roots of my authority.

Motor horn outside.

47

If, on my return this evening, these books are not written fully up to date, I shall ask my committee to request your resignation.

Motor horn sounds again.

Come, Matron, my wife is waiting.

EXEUNT DR. BRAGG *and* MATRON, *Back Centre.*

THOROGOOD

The Chief means it this time, Venner. There's five hours' penmanship before you. You'll enjoy it. (*He grins at Venner.*) Come along, Mary.

MARY

Just a minute.

THOROGOOD (*fond glance*)

I've got to pop into my ward a second. I'll wait for you in the porch.

EXIT THOROGOOD *Back Centre.*

MARY (*earnestly*)

You will do them, won't you, Dr. Venner?

VENNER (*gazing round slowly as though barely aware of her presence*)

I'm not a clerk, am I? You heard him—my unorthodox methods of treatment?

MARY

Yes, it was too unjust.

48

VENNER (*wearily*)

I thought you were on his side.

MARY (*with sudden feeling*)

You're quite worn out.   Really, Dr. Venner, you can't go on killing yourself this way.   Oh, I daresay the work you're doing is brilliant and wonderful, but it isn't worth it, it isn't . . .

VENNER (*looking at her curiously*)

No?

MARY

Not if it brings you to such a state.   You hardly eat these days.   You smoke too much.   You miss your sleep.   You're thinner, much thinner.

VENNER

Why should that worry you?

MARY (*slowly, with painful embarrassment*)

It hurts me to see you so done up . . . and unhappy. That's all.

VENNER

Considering how I've spent my spare time for the last six weeks—your solicitude surprises me.

MARY

I didn't mind what you said.

D   49

VENNER

Is it part of your Christian charity, this forgiveness?

MARY

Perhaps.

VENNER (*sits down at the table, sweeps the case-books to the floor and busies himself with a calculation on his foolscap sheets*)

My head! God! I think I'll chuck this cursed thing for keeps. If only I had a cup of coffee!

MARY's *gaze remains fixed upon him with a strange compassion. She makes up her mind.*

EXIT MARY *Left as* DREWETT ENTERS *Back Centre.*

DREWETT

Why, Venner—still at it?

DREWETT *goes to small table at Back, sits down, takes a pack of cards from the mantelpiece and begins slowly to deal himself a hand of patience.*

By the by, I came past your ward—Foster's missus is looking for you.

VENNER

Oh! (*Working away.*) Don't let our female evangelist see you with those devil's playthings.

DREWETT

You're so hard on that child, Venner. I suspect you of being attracted by her.

50

Don't be a bloody fool. The hydrogen-ion concentration of Na is constant. Oh God! (*He throws down his pencil.*) Drewett, I'm at my last ditch—the chemical standardisation of betrazol—and I just haven't got the legs to jump it.

DREWETT (*placing a card*)

Knock off for a bit.

VENNER (*with fatigued intensity*)

Would you shout that to the jockey when you'd backed his horse? (*He lies back in his chair, slowly lights a cigarette and takes a long inhalation.*) Ah, that's better. You don't know how I miss smoking in there.

DREWETT (*surprised*)

Eh?

For my P-ion synthesis I've been using tri-toluol, which happens to be, in its own quiet way, a high explosive. Limited as your knowledge is, my friend, you realise if I started flinging sparks around I'd blow the roof off. (*Heavily*) God! I do feel bloody low this morning. Bragg's nagging is getting on my nerves. These calculations are hanging in the air. Suppose I don't standardise? Suppose the whole thing's a washout? Hell! I'm almost losing faith in it.

Knock at Door Back Centre.

Yes?

Enter Mrs. Foster. *She is a small spare middle-aged woman of the working class : clean, respectable, resolutely " well-doing ". She carries a basket. The normal determination of her character is not obscured by her present gratitude.*

MRS. FOSTER

I hope you'll excuse the liberty, Dr. Venner. Bein' as Sunday mornin's the only time I can manage, Sister Hall said p'raps you'd see me.

VENNER

Oh, it's you, Mrs. Foster. Come in. What can I do for you?

MRS. FOSTER

No more nor what you're doing, sir. I just seen my Tom. Well!

VENNER

Satisfied?

MRS. FOSTER

You don't know what it means to me, sir. Talked to me, he did, just like his old self. Interested! Askin' for the children. It'll not be long, Martha, he says, before I'm back at the brick-works. A proud day it'll be for me, sir, when he walks out to his job again!

VENNER (*kindly*)

Of course—I'm trying to give your husband a new nervous system, Mrs. Foster—but—you quite realise— no one can give him a new heart.

MRS. FOSTER

You wouldn't trouble about his heart, sir, if you knew the weights he's lifted in his time.

VENNER (*shaking his head*)

That's why I do trouble!

MRS. FOSTER

Now he's sensible he'll soon have his strength back.

VENNER (*hesitant*)

Yes, but . . .

MRS. FOSTER

Did me good this mornin' to see him sittin' up in bed relishin' the little bit o' brawn I fetched him—which reminds me. Could I make so free, sir? (*Takes bowl wrapped in napkin from basket.*) I brought a shape special for you. It's home made—tender as chicken—they do say as how I have a regular hand for it!

VENNER

That's uncommon kind of you, Mrs. Foster.

MRS. FOSTER

With my grateful thanks, sir. (*Putting it on sideboard.*) I can 'ave the bowl next Sunday. I mustn't take up no more of your time. But I did 'ave to pop in like, to say how grateful I am. (*Goes to door.*) You'll not let up on Tom, sir?

VENNER

I'll do all I can.

MRS. FOSTER

Thank you, sir. Good morning, sir. Good morning, Dr. Drewett.

Exit MRS. FOSTER *Back Centre*.

VENNER

Blast! (*Annoyed with himself.*) But how could I tell that poor soul her husband's got a hopeless coronary stenosis!

DREWETT

Poor soul! She's like all the rest of them—a vixen underneath.

VENNER

Oh—rot!

DREWETT

I hope you're not getting sentimental?

VENNER

Do I look it?

DREWETT

Do I? Yet every night for four years I shoved a woman's photograph below my pillow.

VENNER

In the prison camp?

DREWETT (*nods*)

I nearly killed the Russian in the next bed, the poor devil who taught me this patience, for asking if she were my mistress.

VENNER

Wasn't she?

DREWETT

Someone else's (*Pause.*) My wife.

VENNER goes to the sideboard, helps himself to another stiff whisky, drinks it.

VENNER

Drewett, you're about the only person in this place with whom I'm in—shall I say intellectual affinity.

DREWETT

You flatter me.

VENNER

Will you write up these case-books for me?

A perceptible pause. DREWETT, *unseen by* VENNER, *restrains himself.*

DREWETT

What on earth do you take me for? Thirty years ago, outside the divorce courts, I swore I'd done my last good deed.

VENNER

Oh, well! I must do them this afternoon myself. Can't risk being kicked out at this stage.

He bends over the table, lifts his papers, puts his hand to his head and attempts to pick up the thread of his calculations. The church bells make a final crescendo.

Curse those blasted bells! How can I think?

The bells are silent. MARY ENTERS *L. with a tray on which are coffee and some sandwiches. She puts it silently on the table at which* VENNER *sits. He looks up with a jerk.*

What's this?

MARY

You said you would like some coffee. Please drink it. It'll do you good.

VENNER

Little ministering angel.

MARY (*nervously*)

Say what you like . . . only drink the coffee.

VENNER (*his irony has no conviction*)

You'll be late for church. God won't love you any more.

MARY

I'll take my chance.

VENNER

Secure in salvation she braves the storm. Moody and Sankey 999. Any sugar in it?

MARY

Yes.

VENNER (*taking the cup which she pours out and drinking*)

This is good. (*Simply*) Why have I been so beastly to you?

MARY

I don't know.

VENNER

You've never studied the habits of the domestic cuttle-fish?

MARY

No.

VENNER

The wretched little brute shoots his venom—not from malice aforethought—but simply because he's so desperately scared of being hurt.

MARY

I see.

VENNER (*quietly*)

That's by way of an apology. I must chuck ragging you. You're—decent.

MARY

Thank you.

VENNER (*gazing at her oddly*)

And most terribly pretty. Don't let our clean-limbed young Englishman make love to you.

MARY

Who?

VENNER

Thorogood.

57

MARY

He's engaged to be married.

VENNER

A ring makes no difference to an amorous baboon.

DREWETT

Not unless it's worn through the nose!

VENNER (*weary laugh*)

Not bad, papa!

MARY

Do try and get some rest. You need it.

Exit Mary *Back Centre*.

VENNER (*gazing after her*)

She is a sweet little thing. (*Sudden intensity*) I'm inclined to agree—my venerable friend—with your earlier absurdity. (*Thickly*) God! I'm tired! And, oh God! will I ever get that cursed formula complete?

Almost against his will he flings himself on the couch. The next moment his head has fallen back. He is asleep. DREWETT waits a little, then rises quietly. He pulls a rug, that is rolled up at the foot of the couch, over Venner, gazes a moment at the sleeping man, shakes his head gently, then goes back to his patience. As he plays his next card

CURTAIN

The CURTAIN RISES *almost immediately. It is now seven o'clock in the evening of the same day.* VENNER *is still asleep*

58

upon the couch. *The curtains are drawn. One standard lamp with a yellow shade, near the couch, faintly illuminates the room, but throws a strange light upon Venner's upturned face. The case-books have been gathered from the floor and again stand in a neat pile upon the side table. The room is very still.*

Enter Jennie, *with coal-scuttle and tongs. Proceeding to the fireplace she sees that* Venner *is still asleep, assumes a gait of exaggerated precaution and immediately drops the tongs.* Venner *awakes.*

JENNIE

Oh, I'm sorry, sir. I was just going to lay the supper.

VENNER (*getting up stiffly*)

Supper? Have I slept all that time?

JENNIE

You have, sir. You must have wanted it. (*Kneeling down, she begins to make up the fire.*)

VENNER (*sighing*)

Yes, I wanted it. (*He stares moodily at the pile of case-books.*) It's the waking up that's the curse.

JENNIE

Pardon, sir?

VENNER (*rising—bitter tone*)

How neatly you've tidied up all these nice case-books.

JENNIE

That was Dr. Murray's doing, sir.

59

VENNER

Oh! (*He suddenly goes forward and opens one of the case-books.*) My God!

JENNIE

Anything wrong, sir?

VENNER (*turning away*)

No—no.

He moves to the back of the room, leans his head against the mantelpiece. At that moment MATRON *enters, outdoor clothes, Back Centre.*

JENNIE (*immediately stiffening*)

Good evening, Matron. Had a nice day?

MATRON

Very. Why isn't supper laid? I told you we'd be back before seven. Have you made the salad?

JENNIE

Not yet, Matron.

MATRON

Then get on with it.

JENNIE *lifts her tray,* EXITS *hurriedly Left.* MATRON *stands an instant, still unconscious of Venner's presence, then takes a swift step towards the case-books. She takes a rapid glance at them.* VENNER, *watching her, coughs. She turns as if shot.*

Spying on me, eh?

VENNER

For once our positions were reversed.

MATRON (*spiteful*)

I thought you'd do them. I knew that for all your fine talk you'd knuckle under to Dr. Bragg.

VENNER (*in a low voice*)

How you must hate me.

MATRON (*look of great intensity, then evasive*)

I don't hate anybody. . . .

VENNER

Is it because of the room? We can't both have it, Matron.

MATRON (*insidious meekness*)

The room? What room? Oh—you mean your lab.— I admit I spoke rather hasty the other day and I regretted it. It's—it's such a little thing—Dr. Venner. . . .

VENNER (*slowly*)

When you've lived in institutions all your life—don't the little things get big?

MATRON (*dark glance, then a little laugh*)

What queer things you say!

61

VENNER

Perhaps I'm feeling queer tonight. (*Suddenly*) Matron, I don't really mean my stupid jibes—they're only a kind of defence for my own cursed sensitiveness.

MATRON

Oh, Dr. Venner—why should you explain to the likes of me? I'm not a person to bother about. (*Pause.*) You know my parents were in service. Why—(*tortured humility*) I even was myself! Of course, I do my utmost, here—work my fingers to the bone—but the sisters know it and the nurses. Sometimes I catch the probationers laughing behind my back. She was a servant. Imagine! Giving orders!

VENNER

Why don't you—try a change of background?

MATRON

No—No. For all I have to put up with things, I do love it here.

VENNER (*quietly*)

You mean you love Edgar Bragg.

MATRON

What things you say, Dr. Venner! (*Twisting hands together.*) I have the highest feelings towards Dr. Bragg. He's wrapped up in Mrs. Bragg—(*painfully*)—in the lightest movement of her little finger—she's such a nice woman—(*suddenly*) isn't she?

VENNER

Naturally.

MATRON

Yes, I thought you—liked her.

VENNER

Really!

MATRON

Yes, really. (*Softly*) And I know she thinks the world of you.

ENTER MARY *Back Centre.* MATRON's *manner alters. She smiles her false, bright smile.*

Good evening, Dr. Murray. What a lovely day it's been! I must see about supper. As usual, everything gets behind when I am away.

EXIT MATRON L. MARY *half-glances at Venner. She seems confused by his presence and moves towards exit L.*

VENNER

Must you go?

MARY (*awkwardly*)

I'm in no hurry. Do you feel better now?

VENNER

I never feel better.

63

MARY (*quietly*)

That's a pity.

VENNER (*bitterly*)

No—just a matter of principle—with me. (*He sits down at the piano and stares at the keyboard.*) Saves a lot of trouble—and disappointment.

MARY

I'm sorry.

VENNER

Are you? (*He begins mechanically, but softly, to play the first few bars of the Chopin Sonata. She watches him a moment, then goes to door. As her hand touches the door-knob he detains her with a sudden discord.*)

MARY (*turning*)

What's the matter?

VENNER

Nothing—Everything! (*Not looking at her.*) For some strange reason I seem not to want you to go away.

MARY

Oh!

VENNER (*still not looking at her*)

Idiotic—isn't it. (*Pause.*) Why did you do it?

64

MARY

Do what?

VENNER (*rising suddenly from the piano*)

You know what.

MARY (*glances involuntarily at case-books, then averts her head*)

I hope you're not offended. It was little enough . . .
but I told you . . . I wanted—I wanted to help you.

VENNER

To help me! After all my blasted wit at your expense!

MARY (*attempting to smile*)

You know I'm one of those dreadful creatures who keep
turning the other cheek!

VENNER (*intensely*)

Was that why you did it?

MARY (*confused*)

Well—partly.

VENNER (*low voice*)

You're so wonderfully—and so damnably—honest.
(*Pause.*) Mary!

MARY (*still trying to pass it off*)

That's a polite way of calling me a prig.

E

VENNER (*quickly, genuinely*)

No, no! I don't mean it that way! (*Pause, bitterly*) You ought to kick me for this—exhibition.

MARY (*averted head*)

Ought I?

VENNER

It must be—embarrassing for you.

MARY

No, it isn't.

VENNER (*bitterly*)

Well, it is for me. The fact is—I'm not quite my brilliant, dashing self tonight.

MARY

You seem—the same.

VENNER

Possibly. But I feel more like a selfish, surly, self-opinionated swine——

MARY

Oh!

VENNER (*grimly*)

And as this delightful spasm of psycho-analysis can't be in the least amusing for you, I suggest you clear out and leave me to wallow in my ego.

MARY (*slowly*)

You must feel rather down.

VENNER

I feel as though—God! What drivel I'm talking. (*Suddenly, impulsively, reaching out and taking her hand*) Mary, has anyone ever told you how beautiful you are?

MARY (*agitated smile*)

Well—no one who mattered very much.

VENNER

I don't suppose I matter a damn either. But I must tell you. (*Sudden intensity*) You're lovely, Mary, so lovely and so young. You take my breath away. And so good I'm not fit to tie your shoelaces.

MARY

Please don't say that.

VENNER

I oughtn't to—it's such a cursed cliché—but I must. (*Urgently*) Don't you see—I really care—that's why I tried to hurt you!

MARY

You didn't.

VENNER

Then I only hurt myself. Lift your head, Mary. Why,

you're trembling. And I—when I look at you I just—lose myself. As though I were—floating down—into a strange and sunny valley.

MARY (*brokenly*)

I thought you were a scientist—not a poet.

VENNER

I'm nothing—beside you. It's the sudden realisation—like a pain. I'm not lying. It's the truth. Mary, how can I convince you?

MARY (*in a low voice*)

You don't have to.

VENNER (*strangely serious*)

You can't mean it—Mary!—Could you care about me?

MARY (*simply*)

I've loved you from the first moment I saw you. Oh, Paul. I've given myself away. I can't help it. I prayed that you would love me. I've never loved, I'll never love anyone else in all my life.

VENNER

Mary! (*He takes her in his arms.*)

MARY

Paul!

Darling—I feel your heart beating—or is it mine? Nothing else matters . . . now. . . .

Embrace.

DREWETT ENTERS *Back Centre. He observes them and stands curiously still. There is in his face and figure a pained and sad foreboding.*

CURTAIN

ACT II

SCENE: *The Same.*

TIME: *One month later. About three o'clock.*

A lovely spring afternoon. The room is full of sunshine.

> MARY, *in white jacket, stethoscope in pocket, is gaily arranging in vases a large bunch of wild daffodils.*

> THOROGOOD ENTERS *L., rigged out in football shorts, sweater and blazer. He carries a ball under his arm.*

MARY

Aren't they wonderful?

THOROGOOD (*glumly*)

Oh—I suppose so.

MARY (*happily*)

The wood at the end of South Avenue is carpeted with them. I simply had to stop. Like a button-hole?

THOROGOOD (*heavily reproachful*)

Me? Oh, never mind about me. I'm not romantic, I just get on with the job.

MARY (*busy*)

Cheer up. You look quite fetching in those shorts.

70

THOROGOOD

Got to give my chaps a practice before the Blackton match. (*He drops ball on chair, picks up indian clubs.*) I like a man who's fit.

MARY

Do you?

THOROGOOD (*showing off with clubs*)

You don't catch Venner doing this.

MARY (*laughs*)

I don't want to.

THOROGOOD (*stopping clubs*)

Mary, what do you see in the blighter? I suppose you know Foster's taken worse?

MARY

Foster? (*worried.*) He's marvellously improved—quite normal—mentally.

THOROGOOD

Physically he's a wreck.

MARY

Paul can't help it if his heart's bad.

THOROGOOD

Can't he! He can stop these blasted injections.

MARY

What?

THOROGOOD

Betrazol! Huh! It's no use, it's injurious, and Venner's a reckless idiot! If Foster kicks the bucket he'll be in one devil of a——

MARY (*interrupting sharply*)

I won't listen. . . . (*Moves away, passes letter-rack.*) Here! Your letter has arrived.

THOROGOOD (*takes it reluctantly*)

I'll read it later. (*Pause.*) They're all the same!

MARY

Well I never!

THOROGOOD (*hastily*)

I'm not saying a word against Phyllis, she's a grand girl, her pater's my old man's greatest friend. But somehow when you get one every day . . . (*Puts letter in his pocket.*) Walk down with me and watch the practice, Mary.

MARY

I've got to plaster of paris one of my old ladies.

THOROGOOD

Then run into Parchester with me tonight?

MARY (*meaningly*)

Sorry, I'm engaged.

THOROGOOD (*with a rush*)

Mary, you attract me terribly—in fact—if you want to
know—you've quite knocked me over!

MARY (*shortly*)

I'm afraid I don't want to know.

THOROGOOD

But, Mary. . . .

ENTER DREWETT *Back Centre.*

DREWETT

Your team's on the field, Thorogood.

THOROGOOD

Are they? I'll be off, then, at the double. (*Walks
heavily to door, picking up ball.*) By the by, Drewett, the
Chief's coming over this afternoon to discuss arrange-
ments for conference day. I'll be available shortly.

DREWETT (*gravely*)

I'll promise him your advice and co-operation.

THOROGOOD

See you later, Mary.

EXIT THOROGOOD *Back Centre.*

MARY

Where's Paul?

DREWETT

He'll be in presently. He went over to his ward—to give Foster another injection.

MARY (*arrested*)

Another injection!

DREWETT

Yes.

MARY (*troubled*)

Yesterday during rounds I heard Dr. Bragg and Matron—oh, Dr. Drewett—this relapse of Foster's—I'm —I'm worried.

DREWETT

One of the joys of being in love. (*Pause.*) There is always a certain casual drama in a place like this. Don't let it distress you. It's what lies beneath the surface of the pond. . . . (*He shrugs his shoulders significantly.*)

MARY (*oddly startled*)

I don't understand.

DREWETT

The dark little creatures—that twist and turn—unseen in the depths of the human soul.

There is a moment of queer and almost terrifying tension.

MARY (*slowly resuming the rearranging of her flowers*)

I wish Paul and I were away from here.

74

DREWETT

Ah!

MARY

I had a letter from Dr. King yesterday—head of our hospital at Shantchen. They've an outbreak of cerebrospinal amongst the children! When I think of the work we could be doing!

DREWETT (*gazing at her strangely*)

How does Venner react to the—mysterious invocation of the East?

MARY (*puzzled*)

React?

DREWETT

What does he say when you mention China?

MARY (*considering*)

Why . . . I think he usually kisses me.

DREWETT (*flash of humour*)

Strange!

MARY (*slowly*)

Dr. Drewett, I'm terribly happy. I thank God for it every night, on my knees. But somehow—I can't help it—I'm afraid—for Paul.

DREWETT (*about to speak seriously, restrains himself to normal cynicism*)

In spite of the extra milk you give him at lunch-time!

ENTER VENNER *Back Centre, metal case in hand. He is spruce, shaved and well groomed, his white coat clean. His manner is tense and buoyant.*

VENNER

Did I hear the fatal word ' milk '? Bah! (*Smiling.*) Excuse my exuberance, darling. (*Opens case and takes out* 10-c.c. *syringe, begins to clean it.*) I checked my final calculations this morning, grouped my umpteenth titrations, wrote the last word of my thesis. (*Nods R.*) In there—all complete.

MARY

I'm so glad, Paul.

VENNER

The relief! Like having a baby!

DREWETT (*significantly*)

As a happy mother—now you'll think—naturally— about the future.

VENNER (*singing*)

I reck not of the future, father dear!

DREWETT (*going to alcove*)

Levity isn't the soul of wit, Venner. Tut, tut! I've left my new cards upstairs!

MARY (*oddly*)

Aren't you tired of getting it out, Dr. Drewett?

76

DREWETT

I've never got it out. In fact, my friend Boronoff—
who taught it me—predicted dire catastrophe if I ever
did get it out. But he was a gloomy fellow—you know
what these Russians are—he kept trying to hang himself
with his braces.

EXIT DREWETT *L.*

MARY

He's not serious?

VENNER

Couldn't guess it to look at him. Drewett chucked
a top-hole consulting practice in the first month of the
war. Ten days and he was in the front line; another ten
in a prison camp at Laar—Black Forest area—almost
as quick as by Cooks! For four years he admired the
scenery—a brick wall through a window four by two.
Came back, found he'd lost his wife—left her too near an
aerodrome.

MARY (*moved*)

Oh! Not an air raid!

VENNER

An air commodore! Quite broke Drewett! He didn't
even bother to gather up the bits and pieces. Played
patience ever since.

MARY (*frowning*)

How—unjust!

77

VENNER

Reward of a hero! I like the old boy—he hasn't an emotion in his body.

MARY (*pauses, still tense*)

Paul—I don't know what's wrong with me today. I'm—all on edge!

VENNER (*replacing syringe*)

But why?

MARY

Oh—silly ideas, premonitions—it's a strange place here —and a strange sort of life—behind the walls—so shut in— all of us—like a bunch of marionettes on a string.

VENNER

My sweet, you *are* jumpy.

MARY (*sudden resolution*)

One thing anyway, Paul! I'd feel much better— would you—let me give you something?

VENNER

Well—of course!

MARY

I've been screwing up my courage all week. (*Takes a small worn red book from her pocket.*) Whatever you do don't jeer. (*She holds out the book.*)

VENNER (*reading*)

The New Testament.

MARY

It belonged to my father.

VENNER

Oh, no, Mary! I—I don't like the harp—and you'd hate me in a halo!

MARY (*deadly earnest*)

Take it—to please me. At least it's good literature.

VENNER (*pause*)

Oh, all right. (*Makes to pocket it.*)

MARY (*nervous smile*)

Don't treat it like a hot potato.

VENNER

What *does* one do with it?

MARY

Do what my father used to do. Put your finger on a page at random.

VENNER

Mine did that, too. Trying to redeem the family fortunes.

MARY

Please.

79

VENNER (*unwilling*)

Must I take my nasty medicine, doctor? (*Opens Testament, shuts his eyes and places finger on it.*)

MARY

What does it say?

VENNER

Black sheep in the 3.30.

MARY

Don't joke, darling.

VENNER (*reading*)

" Even so, for so it seemed, as heretofore." Well, that's a non-starter.

MARY (*she has to smile*)

Oh, Paul, you're hopeless. But please promise me one thing. Will you read a little of this—occasionally—for my sake?

ENTER DREWETT.

VENNER *puts the Testament in pocket of his coat.* MARY *looks at the clock.*

Goodness! It's nearly three! And I told Sister to have the plaster ready sharp! I must fly.

VENNER

Think of me as you soar through the air.

MARY

If I didn't—I shouldn't soar.

EXIT MARY *Back Centre*.

DREWETT

I must congratulate you, Venner. That child is a picture of happiness.

VENNER

Nice of you to say so.

DREWETT (*calmly*)

Of course, in three months' time you'll have broken her heart.

VENNER (*angrily*)

What the devil do you mean?

DREWETT

Do you propose departing next month with a sun helmet in one hand and a tambourine in the other?

VENNER (*pause*)

No, I don't.

DREWETT

Have you told her so?

VENNER

Of course not!

F   81

DREWETT

Why not?

VENNER (*with supreme irritation*)

Damn it all!   Because I'm in love with her!

DREWETT

Frankly, my dear Venner, as a biologist, you disappoint me.   Weren't you in love with Mrs. Bragg?

VENNER (*vehemently, pacing up and down*)

Good God, no!   Just fool enough to take a sleeping-draught.   Besides—I'm ashamed to say—it amused me to make an ass of Bragg.

DREWETT

He isn't the ass this time.   Don't you realise—you pledged to science—she to God . . . (*Cynically*) No greater incompatibility ever existed since the voice first breathed o'er Eden!

VENNER

I can't help myself, I tell you!   (*Doggedly*) And I still say that I love her.   It'll work out if we give it a chance.

DREWETT

Don't imagine that you'll shake her, she's immovable. As for the other thing, if you are hoping to . . .

VENNER (*furious*)

Shut your mouth!   Oh, I'm sorry, Drewett!

DREWETT (*with a certain melancholy*)

Venner, probably I'm in my dotage—and of course I don't really care a brass farthing either way—but the prospects of this adventure . . . (*He makes appalled gesture.*)

ENTER BRAGG *Back Centre with a pad of notes in his hand. He is followed by* GLADYS.

BRAGG

Where's Matron? (*Looking at his watch*) Ah! Not quite three yet.

GLADYS (*brightly, not looking at Venner*)

Good afternoon, Dr. Drewett.

DREWETT

Afternoon, Mrs. Bragg.

BRAGG (*reading*)

" Reception and lunch at one. Meeting and election at two. Football match at three. Dance at seven o'clock. Full committee meeting under the new president at eleven sharp the following morning. As official hostess, my dear—you may agree it is a comprehensive programme?

GLADYS (*conquering her antipathy*)

Lovely! I'm so excited! (*She laughs.*) Edgar and I have been brushing up our dancing, haven't we, darling?

BRAGG (*immensely gratified*)

Especially the—what's it?—the rumba. I've an excellent sense of rhythm, Drewett. Ta-rum-tum. Ta-rum-tum.

GLADYS (*again to Drewett, strained voice*)
It's such an honour for Edgar!

BRAGG (*beaming chidingly*)
My dear!

GLADYS
I must speak as I feel! (*She goes up to him with stiff pretence of affection, pats his tie in place.*) Now, about the table?

BRAGG (*recollecting*)
Oh, yes—Drewett—we're so short of serving-tables—I thought we might utilise the canterbury in your room.

DREWETT
It's very small.

BRAGG
Every little helps! (*Moving to door L.*) Shall we take a look at it?
EXEUNT BRAGG *and* DREWETT L.

VENNER (*constrained*)
Well, Gladys?

GLADYS (*very still*)
Well?

84

VENNER

You seem—busy?

GLADYS

I do the little I can—for Edgar.

VENNER

I'm sure he appreciates it.

GLADYS

He does.   (*Peculiar glance.*)   He's a demonstrative man.

VENNER

Ah.

GLADYS (*controlling herself, she turns, striving to be quiet and
normal*)

Paul, my dear.   I haven't really seen you for days.
How are you?

VENNER

Still bent on matrimony, but otherwise normal.

GLADYS

I hope—for your own sake—you're not making a
frightful mistake.

VENNER

Marriage is a lottery, as you know, Gladys.

GLADYS

What you can see in her?   Her clothes!—well, I've no

85

vanity; I have to look decent for Edgar's sake. But a psalm-singing schoolgirl! Have you no taste?

VENNER

You thought I had two months ago.

GLADYS (*rising feeling*)

Why must you wound me? You know I'm so easily hurt.

VENNER

I don't want to hurt you, Gladys. Not for anything! Only—we must be philosophical. . . .

GLADYS (*bitterly*)

You weren't so philosophical—some evenings I remember.

VENNER

I'm sorry, Gladys. But I did—from the beginning—try to be honest with you.

GLADYS

How can you talk like that! When I gave you . . . everything!

VENNER (*slight impatience*)

You know you've had other affairs.

GLADYS (*quickly*)

Before we met.

86

VENNER

Please, Gladys—we're both grown up! . . . We were two very bored people—we had an amusing interlude. Now we ought to be the best of friends.

GLADYS (*anguish*)

Friends! (*Impulsively*) Oh, Paul!—I can't believe it's come to this. And I won't. Let's get away from it all. Go abroad. Travel. Lately, I've had such thoughts—such longing for a little place I know—a little gasthaus in Switzerland, high up on the Weisshorn. Let's go there —run away—together—to the snows.

VENNER

What! Oh, be reasonable, Gladys—we'd . . . (*trying to lighten tension*) we'd both get chilblains!

GLADYS (*passionately*)

Don't make a joke of it—let's go away!

VENNER (*shortly*)

I must stay—my lab.'s here.

GLADYS (*carried away*)

Then let me help you—I can make Edgar do things for you, give you more chance for your research. I can do it, Paul.

VENNER

What a charming suggestion!

GLADYS

I'd do anything in the world for you—if only you'd come back to me!

VENNER (*patiently*)

Don't you see, I can't.

GLADYS

At least—(*desperately*) say you love me.

VENNER (*as kindly as he can*)

But I don't love you, Gladys, and you know I never did.

There is a silence. Her pride is lacerated beyond endurance, but she recovers herself.

GLADYS (*tremulous laugh*)

I don't care. I was only pretending—to see how we stood. If you offered me your undying passion I'd throw it in your face.

VOICES *off Left.* ENTER BRAGG *and* DREWETT, *Left, in conversation.*

BRAGG

You'll be delighted, my dear—the table is suitable. Why, what's the matter?

GLADYS

Nothing, Edgar. The room is a little warm.

BRAGG

Open the window, Venner.

VENNER *does so.*

VENNER

You won't want me any more, will you, Dr. Bragg?

BRAGG (*looking up from his pad of notes*)

What? (*brusquely*) Oh, no—no.

VENNER *goes to the door of his laboratory R., takes the key from his pocket, puts it in the lock.*

ENTER MATRON *Back Centre.*

MATRON

Just a minute, Dr. Venner. (*There is something compelling in her voice.*) I'm sorry I'm late, Dr. Bragg. You know I do my utmost to be punctual. But Sister Hall sent for me. (*Pause.*) There's been a dreadful emergency in Dr. Venner's ward.

VENNER

My ward!

MATRON (*paying no attention to him*)

A terrible thing has happened, Dr. Bragg. Five minutes ago Foster collapsed. . . .

VENNER (*loudly*)

Foster! Why wasn't I sent for?

89

MATRON

Because he's dead.

VENNER

Dead! (*He pushes past Matron.*)

DREWETT

Wait, Venner.

EXIT VENNER *Back Centre.* DREWETT *follows him.*

MATRON (*immobile*)

There was no time to do anything. Dr. Venner gave the injection at half-past two. Just afterwards Foster sat up and asked for a drink of water. Before Sister Hall could get to him he fell back, dead.

BRAGG

Good heavens! (*Taken aback, undecided.*) I—I'd better get to the ward at once.

MATRON

If I might take the liberty, Dr. Bragg—isn't it beneath your dignity to go running to the ward?

BRAGG

Yes, yes . . . perhaps you're right, Matron.

MATRON (*very still and quiet*)

After all, Dr. Venner is entirely to blame.

BRAGG (*startled*)

Eh?

90

MATRON

We all know you've been against this—this experimenting from the start. You said it was dangerous, that you'd hold Dr. Venner responsible. Isn't that so, Mrs. Bragg?

GLADYS

Yes. . . . (*Coming slowly forward*) You did, Edgar.

BRAGG

My dear!

GLADYS

If you hush this up, it might ruin your career—they'd say you were to blame. They'd never make you President.

BRAGG (*choking*)

I!—why—why, I virtually forbade Dr. Venner to continue this treatment.

GLADYS

I know you did. But he's always gone out of his way to defy you.

BRAGG

But I—I thought you liked Venner.

GLADYS

What an idea!

THOROGOOD *bursts in Back Centre.*

THOROGOOD

Have you heard, sir? Isn't it shocking?

BRAGG (*raising authoritative hand*)

I'm handling this, Thorogood.

GLADYS

You must protect yourself, Edgar. You mustn't let him go on with his research work.

BRAGG

I'll stop it immediately!

MATRON

Oughtn't you to close up his laboratory, Dr. Bragg? Look, the key's in the door, there.

BRAGG

Oblige me, Matron, by securely locking the door.

MATRON *does so.*

Also by keeping possession of that key.

As MATRON *pockets the key* VENNER ENTERS *Back Centre. He comes in briskly. For a moment there is silence in the room.*

VENNER

Yes . . . quite right . . . he's gone, poor chap.

BRAGG

We're already aware of that unhappy fact.

VENNER

Coronary stenosis. Query embolism. The P.M. should be interesting—besides giving me sections of his cerebrum. Why are you looking at me like that?

THOROGOOD

The Chief isn't satisfied. None of us are.

VENNER

What? It was a perfectly natural death . . . an intercurrent cardiac affair . . . the post mortem'll show it.

BRAGG (*heatedly*)

Have I given you permission to do a P.M.?

VENNER

No, but you will.

BRAGG (*fuming*)

How dare you anticipate my actions?

VENNER (*breaking out*)

What the hell's all the fuss about? You don't really give a damn about Foster—he was only one of your charity boys.

BRAGG

You're insulting, sir. But never mind. We're going to find out if your treatment was the cause of this man's death.

VENNER

Don't be funny. Betrazol has no thrombotic action whatsoever.

BRAGG (*pompous rage*)

Far be it from me to pit my knowledge against a mind like yours. Nevertheless I find it my duty to bring this case, and all that pertains to it, to the notice of the committee.

VENNER

What do your hand-picked bunch of muddleheads know about scientific research?

BRAGG

You may find out.

VENNER

You only co-opt them to take the proprietary label off this place!

BRAGG

I shall convey to them your opinion of their abilities. Meanwhile I'm going to 'phone the coroner.

VENNER

The coroner! (*Pause.*) It'll be all the more painful for you in the end. Don't you understand—oh, God!— what's the use? But think it over before you make a fool of yourself.

He turns abruptly to the door R., tries it, finds it locked, fumbles for his key in various pockets.

94

BRAGG

You won't get in there, Dr. Venner.

VENNER (*turning*)

Where's my key?

BRAGG

It's not your key, Dr. Venner. It's the key of a room in my establishment.

VENNER

You can't close my laboratory.

BRAGG

I have closed it. And closed it must remain until the committee's inspection!

VENNER (*advancing*)

Give me that key.

BRAGG (*hastily*)

I haven't got it.

VENNER

Who has? (*Glancing furiously round.*) Fanny! You bitch!

THOROGOOD

Don't be a cad, Venner, or I'll knock you down.

VENNER (*withering look*)

It's all so damned childish. It makes no odds now if

the lab. is locked for a couple of days. (*He turns away, sits down on piano stool.*)

BRAGG

You'll be given the opportunity to collect your material at the proper time.

VENNER

That's British! (*He plays first few bars of " Land of Hope and Glory ".*)

BRAGG

Insolence won't help you, Venner. Dr. Thorogood, Matron, we will continue our conference in my office. Come, Gladys!

EXIT BRAGG *Back Centre, followed by* MATRON *and* THOROGOOD. *As they file out* VENNER *loudly plays Blake's Grand March.*

VENNER (*stops playing*)

Aren't you glad you didn't go to Switzerland?

GLADYS (*low voice*)

You've got plenty of time to change your mind.

VENNER (*bitterly*)

What a hope!

BRAGG (*fondly, through window*)

Gladys!

GLADYS

I'm coming, Edgar.

VENNER (*yodelling*)

La-la-la-e-tee.

EXIT GLADYS *Back Centre.* *When she has gone* VENNER *drops his pretence of unconcern.* *He sits, rather tensely, thinking.*

ENTER DREWETT *Back Centre.*

DREWETT

That's done, then.   I've had him taken over.

VENNER

Will you give me a hand with the P.M. ?

DREWETT (*amazed*)

You can't do it today?

VENNER

I'm damn well going to!

DREWETT

But—that's impossible—you must get the consent of the relatives—comply with the formalities.

VENNER (*tensely*)

Drewett! Why do you think I chose Foster as the first recipient of betrazol? Not only because I wanted to restore the poor chap's mind while he *was* here—but because I knew that only too soon he would provide me with pathological evidence—to support my thesis.

DREWETT (*comprehending*)

Sections showing the effect of your preparation?

VENNER

Exactly. (*Strung up.*) Now Bragg has the bit between his teeth—he's already closed my lab., he'll obstruct me in every way, insist on doing the resection himself. You know his technique! (*Loudly*) How can I risk him botching these vital specimens?

DREWETT

I see!—of course—it's none of my business.

VENNER (*nervous violence*)

Don't you want to help me?

DREWETT

No. (*Pause.*) But for purely scientific reasons—when do you want to start?

VENNER

Soon as you get away from settling the strength of the conference claret cup. Have you the key of the mortuary?

DREWETT *nods.*

Then keep it. They're liable to pinch that, too.

DREWETT (*moving to door*)

I'll be back in half-an-hour.

ENTER MARY *Back Centre.*

MARY (*quickly*)

Paul, dearest! (*She comes rapidly forward, her expression concerned, loving.*) I've just heard—I'm so sorry. . . .

EXIT DREWETT *Back Centre.*

VENNER

Don't look as if I'd just been interred, darling. It's nothing. Only the damned impertinence of the thing.

MARY

I know, dear.

VENNER

Trouble is, they're so ignorant. That's inevitable, I suppose—no scientist is ever recognised in his lifetime by the vulgar herd. But it's dangerous. If Bragg gets me chucked out . . . (*A sudden thought draws him up*)— why—every hospital in the country would shut down on me!

MARY (*gently*)

Would that matter so very much, my dearest?

VENNER

Matter? If I don't get a lab.? And have to give up this one?

MARY

But, Paul! Shan't we be leaving here soon in any case?

VENNER (*starting, then subsiding*)

Oh! I see!

MARY

You know, dear, I believe that everything happens for the best, perhaps even this.

VENNER

Then everything in the garden's lovely!

MARY

Paul!

VENNER

Mary, dearest, you don't really want me to come out to Shantchen?

There is a silence.

MARY

You said you would come with me . . . you said . . . (*whispering*) to the ends of the earth.

VENNER

I'm quite capable of spouting poetry when in the mood.

MARY (*hurt*)

Oh, my dear. . . .

VENNER

I'd do anything rather than hurt you, Mary. But you know what my work means to me?

MARY

Yes, I do!

VENNER

Then you couldn't want me to chuck it?

MARY

No, no. You'd find a splendid lab. at Shantchen.

VENNER (*exasperated*)

I might find one in Tibet! But I couldn't work with the Grand Llama intoning down my neck—oh, Mary! Why must you try to drag me out!

MARY

Sometimes a woman sees more clearly than a man—especially if she loves him!

VENNER (*impatient*)

Darling! That's such a platitude!

MARY (*stubborn*)

Platitudes can be true!

VENNER (*angry*)

Then let's have a string of them.   You want to make a new man of me, save me, set me on the straight and narrow path!

MARY

I want us to be happy.   And we won't be for long—unless we have something in common—spiritually.

VENNER

Don't you love me?

MARY

Terribly.

VENNER

Then what more do we want? I love you and I'm willing to marry you.

MARY

Willing to . . . ?

VENNER (*going to her*)

Curse it, I'm saying everything the wrong way. I'm crazy about you.   But you must give up—this wild idea!

MARY

My wild idea is as important to me as yours is to you.

VENNER

I daresay. But I think mine more important to mankind.

MARY

Oh, my dear, is it—is it? Can't you see beyond the bottom of a test tube—the end of a microscope? What has all your science done for the world—with its aeroplanes, poison gas and machine guns? Only brought it to ruin! If they find a way to split the atom they'll only use it to make a new explosive! But the things I believe in— they'd save the world. People blame God or deny Him, because of the awful state we're in today. They forget that all this ghastly muddle comes from man's utter disobedience and neglect of the rules of life God gave us! What can we expect if we worship machines instead of our Creator!

VENNER

You can't prove that God exists.

MARY

Why should I—when He proves it, every day, to me?

VENNER

He's never given me much proof!

MARY

Dearest, for all your cleverness, you're like a stubborn

schoolboy! Don't you see, you must fulfil certain con-
ditions—only those who set out to seek Him will find
Him! You can't make a friend without going half-way—
offering some personal response. . . .

VENNER (*sudden bitterness*)

I don't have friends—only enemies, it seems.

MARY

Oh, Paul, I don't want to preach at you—but if only
you'd lift your eyes up—you'd realise—material things
don't count—Even you and I——

VENNER (*interrupting*)

Naturally I can't set myself up in competition with the
Saviour.

MARY (*quietly*)

Paul, you terrify me when you talk like that!

VENNER

It's all a fairy tale to me, Mary.

MARY

You can't deny historical fact. Christ preached on
this earth, performed miracles—that can't be explained
away—died and rose again. . . .

VENNER

I don't believe it!

MARY (*growing intensity*)

He was seen after His death by unimpeachable witnesses
—men who couldn't lie—He even appeared to Thomas—
who doubted Him so much!

VENNER

A visual hallucination! (*Angrily*) What's the use of
talking?—the whole thing's bosh to me.

MARY

Well! (*firmly*) Suppose it was! Suppose it *is* all bosh!—
Miracles, divinity, everything! The fundamentals of
Christianity still remain.

VENNER (*startled*)

Eh? (*Bitter smile.*) You want me to be a Christian
without believing in Christ?

MARY

I want you to believe in service, in self-sacrifice, in some
higher force.

VENNER

I see! The old humanity angle.

MARY

Why not?

VENNER

Well! I'm just not there! I do my work because I'm interested in science—pure science. I don't give a damn for humanity. And your basic idea—that idea of sacrifice —dying of love for someone else—it simply leaves me cold.

MARY (*tears in her eyes*)

I'm sorry you feel like that about it, my dear. (*Sudden passion*) Oh, how can I convince you! I love you so much it breaks my heart to feel that we're apart.

VENNER (*sombrely*)

As you're such good pals with the Almighty you might ask Him to do something about it.

MARY

Yes, that's far truer than you think. I can ask God to help and I will—Oh, Paul, I will ask Him.

ENTER DREWETT *Back Centre, carrying two white gowns, rubber apron and thick red rubber gloves.*

DREWETT

Are you ready?

VENNER

I shall want some formalin for the sections.

DREWETT

It's there.   And the absolute alcohol.

VENNER

Then let's go before Bragg weighs in with the coroner.

MARY

What are you going to do?

VENNER (*sombrely*)

Perform the only real miracle! Resurrect the truth—
from the dead.

EXEUNT DREWETT *and* VENNER.

MARY *stands alone, emotionally overwrought, then, on an
impulse, she clasps her hands, lifts up her head as if in prayer.*

GLADYS ENTERS. *Her manner, though restrained, is
agitated.*

GLADYS

Oh! . . . I've disturbed you?

MARY (*not turning, hiding her distress*)

It's all right.

GLADYS

I'm sorry—to see you so upset. It's quite absurd of me—but I—I came over—half hoping I might help you.

MARY

How can you help me?

GLADYS

Oh, I don't know! And of course—you'd resent my interference—it's really unpardonable. Still——

MARY (*swinging round*)

Please say what you mean.

GLADYS

Well—it's you and Dr. Venner. (*Great difficulty*) Oh I suppose I shouldn't say it—but—well—you're so young —so inexperienced . . . and marriage—isn't it a big price to pay for one's first infatuation?

MARY (*slowly*)

This isn't infatuation.

GLADYS

That's what I thought when I was your age. But afterwards—one finds out. (*Quickly*) And then—you'd both be so unhappy!

MARY

No, no—we won't. Besides—I'd rather be miserable with him than . . .

GLADYS (*breaking in*)

I knew you'd say that—it shows how completely you've been swept off your feet. But—just think for a minute— what do you know about Dr. Venner?

MARY

Enough to make me love him.

GLADYS (*suppressed jealousy breaking through*)

Yes, he'd see to that! I've watched you in the evenings —walking down the avenue—close to him. (*Sudden pang*) You shouldn't go out with him so late—it isn't right!

MARY

I've done nothing I'm ashamed of!

GLADYS

No—but still—(*strained voice*) when he kisses you, takes you in his arms . . .

MARY (*upset*)

I don't know what you mean. But I won't hear——

GLADYS (*quickly*)

I'm saying nothing against him. He's brilliant, he's charming. (*Pause.*) But he's not your sort. He'll only jeer at everything you hold dear!

MARY

No, no, he won't.

GLADYS

Later on he will.

MARY

How cruel you are!

GLADYS

You've got your mission, your vocation. Don't you ever wake up in the middle of the night wondering—if you're not betraying the very cause you've dedicated your life to!

MARY (*increased distress*)

It can't be wrong—to love someone. . . .

GLADYS

And when you're lying awake—in the stillness—doesn't your conscience keep on and on—telling you to stamp out this unworthy affection—renounce it—make a great sacrifice—for God?

MARY (*wildly*)

God couldn't want me to give him up.

GLADYS (*swiftly*)

You only say that because it's hard. If you let him go his way—and went yours—you'd find happiness—such happiness—in renunciation—in crushing your own heart.

MARY (*distractedly*)

Why are you saying all this to me?

GLADYS

I suppose I'm utterly selfish. And yet—in some queer way—I like you.

MARY (*intensely*)

It's more . . . than that.

GLADYS

No, no. I'm only thinking of what's best for everyone.

MARY

For everyone. (*Stunned, seeing something in Gladys' eyes*) Oh, no . . . No! . . . not you!

111

GLADYS (*about to deny, then sees it useless—flat voice*)
Why not? It only shows that what I say is true. If you hadn't come—he'd still have been—my lover.

The two stand looking at each other.

CURTAIN

ACT II

SCENE II

SCENE: *The Same.*

TIME: *About half-past six on the evening of Wednesday, April 14th, first day of the conference at Hopewell Towers.*

> *The curtains are drawn, all lights on. At the small table in the alcove* DREWETT, *without jacket, showing boiled shirt, black tie and braces, sits finishing a game of patience.*

> ENTER THOROGOOD *Left, very red and shiny, in full dress clothes.*

THOROGOOD (*bursting with the news*)

Well!—now there's hell to pay!

DREWETT

Oh?

THOROGOOD

I was in the Chief's office—he was asking me to stand by for the Mayor and other distinguished guests—when who do you think barged in? (*Goes to sideboard and begins to mix himself a drink.*)

DREWETT (*shortly*)

I have no idea! Give me a whisky and soda, will

you? A stiff one! Your uncle's presidential address today—wonderful—but I'm not so young as I was!

THOROGOOD (*handing drink*)

It was Mrs. Foster!

DREWETT

Indeed!

THOROGOOD

You ought to have heard her—my God!—it was a treat. (*Suddenly*) Look here, Drewett, what *did* Venner find at the P.M.?

DREWETT

Why don't you ask him?

THOROGOOD

I have!

DREWETT (*playing card*)

What did he say?

THOROGOOD

What do you think?

DREWETT

Yes—I'm afraid you'll have to wait till it's thrashed out before the committee tomorrow.

THOROGOOD (*laughs*)

The committee! It's going slightly further! Believe me, our scientific friend's got it coming to him! And serve him right! He's too damned cock-a-hoop for my taste.

DREWETT (*slowly*)

I don't think he's been especially cock-a-hoop these last few days.

MATRON ENTERS *Back Centre.*

THOROGOOD (*genial*)

Glass of sherry?

MATRON

Well, just this once. Seeing Dr. Bragg was so kind as to send over the wine.

THOROGOOD (*handing her a glass*)

Your good health, Matron!

MATRON

We ought to drink Dr. Bragg's health. What a day this has been for him! (*Rapt expression*) I turned quite giddy—when the chairman stood up in Great Hall and announced that Dr. Bragg had been chosen—out of all the doctors in Great Britain and Northern Ireland—as President of the Psychological Association.

DREWETT (*bending over his cards*)

How the patients cheered!

MATRON (*darting a suspicious glance at Drewett*)

How everyone cheered!

THOROGOOD

Our respected Chief!

MATRON *and he drink.*

ENTER VENNER *Back Centre. He is still in a lounge suit. His manner is hard and bitter.*

(*Stiffly*) Hum-hum! That you, Venner?

VENNER

I think so.

THOROGOOD

Have a drink?

VENNER

What! And me just taken the pledge! (*He mixes himself a whisky.*) Good God! Is this our worthy Matron indulging in a wild debauch?

MATRON

I've had one glass of wine (*spitefully*) to drink to Dr. Bragg's election.

VENNER

Tut, tut! Don't you know that fermented liquors make the nose red?

MATRON

Will you let me alone, Dr. Venner?

VENNER

And there's spontaneous combustion! Your alcoholic expirations—Edgar's rumba heated passion!

MATRON (*rigid with hatred*)

You'll pay for this!

VENNER

Think of the tragedy—if you went off 'pop'—all over the new president's best shirt front. (*Drinking*) Best respects.

MATRON (*inarticulate*)

You . . . you beast!

By a tremendous exercise of will MATRON *takes herself in hand, gives Venner a long look.* EXIT R.

DREWETT (*studying cards*)

This hand—it's remarkable!

THOROGOOD (*blandly*)

I've a small spot of news for you, Venner.

VENNER

Oh! (*Moving restlessly about, glass in hand.*) Don't say your fiancée's coming tonight?

THOROGOOD

Er—no, it isn't that!

VENNER

Ah!

THOROGOOD

What d'you mean, " ah "?

VENNER

Nothing. Just ah! It does seem a sell to lead that poor girl a paperchase all the year round if you don't show her a good time once in a while.

THOROGOOD

Oh, shut up—it's—it's too far for her to come!

DREWETT (*excited*)

Be quiet, both of you! This thing—it's actually threatening to come out.

VENNER (*moving across, fidgeting with Drewett's cards*)

That ten goes on the knave.

DREWETT

I was about to put it there.

VENNER

And the queen on the king.

118

DREWETT

For heaven's sake, Venner!

VENNER

Sorry, sorry!

DREWETT

I need a black ten.

VENNER

There!

DREWETT

I believe—no, it's impossible!

VENNER

Keep cool!

DREWETT

I'm stuck! I want a red nine—I'm done.

VENNER (*playing card*)

Here!

DREWETT

Good heavens!

VENNER (*playing*)

And the eight of clubs.

119

DREWETT (*playing*)

Seven, five, four, three. No, I can't believe it—yes, it's—it's the two!

VENNER (*turning last card*)

And the ace!

DREWETT

Out! At last!

THOROGOOD

Well, I'm blowed!

DREWETT (*rising, curiously disturbed*)

That's strange. Tonight—(*looks at Venner*)—somehow. . . . (*Shakes his head, queer foreboding.*)

THOROGOOD (*crudely*)

Lucky at cards unlucky in love. (*Guffaws.*) Drewett—you'll never bag another wife now!

DREWETT (*moving away*)

Thank you for reminding me! But, as usual—you rather miss the point!

He EXITS *L.*

THOROGOOD (*staring after Drewett*)

What the hell's wrong with everybody tonight?

VENNER

You'd never know.   Your hide's too goddamned thick!

THOROGOOD

Yeh? Well, yours better be. Let me tell you . . .

Knock at door Back Centre.

Come in.

Enter Mrs. Foster *Back Centre, nervous, but burning with deep sense of injury.*

Mrs. Foster

Dr. Venner?

Venner

Well?

Mrs. Foster

Dr. Bragg said I could 'ave a word with you.

Venner

Ah! (*Quietly*) Make it short, then, please. I've got to change for the dance.

Mrs. Foster

Dance, indeed! With my poor Tom cold and stiff in his coffin!

Venner (*quietly sympathetic*)

Can I help it?

Mrs. Foster

That's what I want to know!

VENNER

Look here, Mrs. Foster. What has Dr. Bragg been saying to you?

MRS. FOSTER

He's too much of a gentleman to say what's in his mind—but I can tell—though I am only a poor workin' woman. (*Loud*) You didn't ought to have cut my Tom about, Dr. Venner.

VENNER

I've already explained, Mrs. Foster—I simply had to have these sections, early, for scientific reasons—for the benefit of thousands of other sick people like your husband.

MRS. FOSTER

What benefit did 'e get out of it? (*Louder*) You should have 'ad my consent—written out legal—Dr. Bragg told me himself.

VENNER (*exasperated*)

What's he got to do with it?

MRS. FOSTER

He's a J.P.! I trust him. He 'asn't done anything underhand or suspicious.

VENNER

Are you inferring that I have?

122

MRS. FOSTER

I don't make no charges. Not 'ere. Dr. Thorogood'll be my witness. But I'm going to 'ave my rights.

VENNER

What rights? Why are you so changed to me?

MRS. FOSTER

I admit that you took me in at the beginning. But there's other doctors in the world. (*Looks at Thorogood.*) Isn't that so, sir?

THOROGOOD

Oh, quite, quite, Mrs. Foster.

MRS. FOSTER (*significant nod, still to Thorogood*)

I swear I know what you're thinking, doctor.

THOROGOOD

You mustn't ask me *that*, Mrs. Foster. Medical etiquette.

VENNER (*angrily*)

For heaven's sake! What are you driving at?

MRS. FOSTER (*tossing head*)

You won't shout me down, Dr. Venner. I know how I stand. And—since you ask me—out with it I will! I'm not satisfied over my husband's treatment!

123

VENNER

I did everything humanly possible!

MRS. FOSTER

Inhumanly, I say—with your butchery! What's more, if a mistake *was* made you couldn't 'ave chose a better way to cover it!

VENNER

Good God!

MRS. FOSTER

You may well say it! For I warn you—now I'm goin' to take steps.

VENNER

I see.

MRS. FOSTER

Since I seen Dr. Bragg my mind's made up. (*Moving towards door*) I'm going to the Parchester police-office—now.

VENNER

Well—(*pause*)—go.

MRS. FOSTER

I am. I shall 'ave my rights if it's the last thing I do!
  EXIT MRS. FOSTER *Back Centre*.

THOROGOOD

Whew! I told you, Venner. (*Assumed condolence*) Damned sorry for you, old chap.

VENNER (*bitter*)

That helps—terribly! (*As he* GOES OUT) Put not your trust in relatives!

EXIT VENNER *Left*.

Elevated, THOROGOOD *mixes himself another drink.*

ENTER MARY *Back Centre*.

THOROGOOD (*effusively*)

Hello! The little person I'm looking for. A spot of sherry before you dress?

MARY

No, thank you. (*She moves toward door L.*)

THOROGOOD

Don't run away. Here's that snap I took of you last week. (*Hands it to her. She looks, quickly, completely unresponsive.*) The boy friend clicks a nifty shutter—what? You're so awfully pretty, Mary, you ought to be better appreciated.

MARY (*putting snapshot on mantelpiece and turning*)

I don't quite know what you mean.

THOROGOOD

We all realise how keen you are to go out there. He'll never go with you!

MARY (*stiffly*)

Won't he?

THOROGOOD

Even if he dodges being struck off the register—oh,
I won't run the blighter down behind his back—but
he's not cut out for that sort of life.

MARY (*cuttingly*)

What do you know about it?

THOROGOOD

I remember a bloke coming down to talk to us at
school. Just home from Burma or some place—a
regular sahib! Lord! He did make me want to go—
right to the outposts of the Empire!

MARY (*moving away coldly*)

It's a pity you didn't.

THOROGOOD (*with a rush*)

But I would. I'd come out with you, stand by you.
I'd be a damned useful man in a tight corner, Mary!

MARY

Aren't you forgetting something?

THOROGOOD

No, no—I realise—Phyllis—but rather than spoil
both our lives—better to have a clean sharp cut.

MARY (*quietly*)

What a bad surgeon you'd have made!

THOROGOOD

But, Mary—I'm decent—it's better to be honest—I've absolutely fallen for you . . . (*He grabs her wrist.*)

MARY

Please let me go.

THOROGOOD

We've so much in common, we go to church together, Phyllis would get over it—I love you, I love you. . . .

MARY (*pulling herself free*)

You're either very stupid or very cruel. I'll try to forget this has ever happened.

ENTER DREWETT L., *wearing jacket of his dinner suit.*

THOROGOOD (*sulky pause*)

You'll be sorry—that's all I say.

DREWETT

It's quite chilly tonight, we should have had the fire. (*He gazes from one to the other.*) Will you spare one dance tonight for a moth-eaten old gentleman?

MARY

No, but I'll dance with you with pleasure, Dr. Drewett.

DREWETT

Thank you.

Sound of a car.

Hadn't we better be getting over, Thorogood, to meet your friend, the mayor?

THOROGOOD (*moving to door*)

To hell with the mayor!

EXEUNT DREWETT *and* THOROGOOD *Back Centre.*

MARY, *still much upset, sits down at desk, takes a sheet of notepaper, begins, slowly, despondently, to write.*

VENNER, *in dinner-jacket,* ENTERS.

VENNER (*tensely*)

Mary, I've been looking for you all afternoon.

MARY (*equal strain, not looking up*)

I was at the Conference.

VENNER (*bitterly*)

That pantomime!

Pause. MARY *goes on writing.*

Well! Have you nothing to say?

MARY

What can I say!

VENNER

Anything! Anything! Don't sit writing letters with this hell between us.

MARY (*slowly*)

It isn't a letter.   (*Pause.*)   It's my resignation.

VENNER

Your *what?*

MARY

I'm confirming what I told Dr. Bragg this afternoon.
(*Utter despondency.*)   I'm leaving for the mission one
month from today.

VENNER

Mary! You can't!

MARY

I must!

VENNER (*bitterly*)

The supreme sacrifice!

MARY

Oh, Paul, why must you jeer?

VENNER

Because I feel like jeering—such waste and futility!

MARY (*stiffly*)

Don't make it harder for us both.

She puts resignation in envelope, leaves it on table.

VENNER (*nervous violence*)

Darling! Why can't you stay—and work for God at home?

MARY (*near to tears*)

You'd laugh at me, at all that I hold sacred—like you laughed at me just now.

VENNER

I swear to heaven I wouldn't.

MARY

You don't believe in heaven.

VENNER (*great strain*)

Are we talking theology—or in love with one another?

MARY

You know I love you. (*Sadly*) But now I wonder . . .

VENNER (*interrupting*)

I do love you. When you come into the room every cell in my body sits up and takes notice.

MARY (*suddenly facing him*)

Is that altogether a new sensation for you?

VENNER (*Pause*)

So Gladys has been talking—I thought she would! Mary! It was nothing—nothing—beside my love for you.

For the first time in my life I know the meaning of the word. I really love you. (*Pause.*) Only—I can't—can't follow at your heels to China!

MARY

Oh, Paul, you're so unfair!

VENNER

It's you who are unfair! Other women have given up their careers for marriage.

MARY

You call it a career!

VENNER

What does it matter what I call it? So long as we don't throw away something that may never come to us again. Oh, Mary—at least let's have our moment— it isn't much out of your eternity.

MARY (*faintly*)

I can't be untrue to myself.

VENNER

Why fight against it, Mary? You're a doctor, you know we've got bodies.

MARY

I know we've got souls!

VENNER

Oh! For God's sake, darling!

MARY

It is for God's sake! And our own!

VENNER (*hopeless gesture*)

Our own! You don't really care a damn!

MARY

How can you say such things? I'd do anything—I'd die for you. . . .

VENNER

Is that necessary?

MARY

Go on!

VENNER

No, no! I don't want to hurt you!

MARY

If you only knew—how my heart's been breaking for you—especially since you've been in this trouble!

VENNER (*quickly*)

That's nothing!

MARY

It's terrible! You don't know how I've lain awake

these last nights—dreading what they would do to you. . . . (*Moves slowly towards table.*)

VENNER

I don't want your pity.

MARY

It isn't—pity. (*Brokenly*) It's such a feeling—all mixed up and terrible—I can't resist it!

A pause. She is at the table.

(*Blindly*) Paul—would you—would you be kind to me—if I stayed?

VENNER

How can you doubt it?

She takes her resignation and tears it up.

Mary! Darling!

MARY

Oh, Paul! (*Desperately*) I couldn't give you up. I must stay. Now, especially, when you need me!

VENNER

I couldn't live without you.

MARY (*breathless*)

For a minute—I had such a pain—here—in my side.

They are, suddenly and irresistibly, in each other's arms.

VENNER

Dearest! I've longed for you so terribly.

133

MARY

You do love me?

VENNER

I adore you.

GLADYS ENTERS *quickly Back Centre. She is smartly dressed in a low evening gown, a light wrap over her shoulders. She stands at the doorway.*

GLADYS (*hand against her side*)

I've come at the wrong time, it seems.

MARY (*low voice*)

I'll go now, Paul. . . .

VENNER

No, wait, darling.

MARY (*going L.*)

I'll see you later—in the hall.

MARY EXITS *L.*

GLADYS (*uncertain, struggling with her jealousy*)

I wondered if I'd run over. I thought no, then—I thought I might. (*Advancing*) I'm—I'm not really a vindictive woman, Paul!

VENNER (*still tense with emotion*)

Aren't you?

GLADYS

I—I thought you might like to see my dress. I just had a minute before the dance begins. It's quite the latest. D'you like it?

VENNER (*not looking*)

It's all right!

GLADYS (*her expression changing*)

Let me tell you it's a million times smarter than the dowdy rags she wears—

VENNER (*outburst*)

For pity's sake! What do clothes matter at a time like this!

GLADYS

Don't let's argue, Paul. I want to be friends. Will you dance with me tonight?

VENNER

I shan't be dancing much.

GLADYS

But you must! Then we can talk about things. I'm sorry, Paul, about—everything. I—I was so furious, I know I egged Edgar on—but if you come over—we might straighten it all out.

VENNER (*wearily*)

Haven't we been into this before?

GLADYS

But not the way things are now.   (*Eagerly*) She's going,
Paul?   I heard so, from Edgar, today.

VENNER

He's naturally inaccurate.

GLADYS (*pleading*)

Oh, Paul!—my dear!

VENNER (*his nerves getting the better of him*)

Will you stop!   I've put up with your confounded
possessiveness long enough!

GLADYS (*sudden temper*)

Be careful, Paul!   I've got my pride!   I won't have
you turn me down a second time.

VENNER

Go to hell!

GLADYS (*enraged*)

You can't speak to me like that!

VENNER (*driven beyond endurance*)

Can't I?   Don't you realise I'm sick of you, I hate the
sight of you?

GLADYS

How dare you!

136

VENNER

You—you disgust me!

GLADYS (*hands clenched*)

How dare you! How dare you!

VENNER

That's how I feel about you.

Exit Venner *Back Centre.* Gladys *stands, in a passion of rage and humiliation.*

Enter Matron, *dressed for the dance. She observes Gladys intently.*

MATRON (*curious tone*)

Dr. Venner carries things off well, doesn't he?

GLADYS (*suppressed voice*)

Too well.

MATRON

Nothing ever downs him. He seems head over heels in love with Dr. Murray, too. Beautiful little thing, isn't she? The other evening when I came in—there they were—kissing each other, in one another's arms—close, hugging—well!

GLADYS (*trembling*)

Dr. Venner'll make a big mistake one day.

MATRON (*with a little laugh*)

That's what everyone's been saying for years, but he's just the kind that slips out of everything.

137

Wait till tomorrow. Wait till my husband—wait till they *all* start on him. I'd like to see his face when they dismiss him, kick him out, send him . . .

MATRON (*interrupting, great reasonableness*)

I wouldn't be so sure, Mrs. Bragg. He's clever! (*Sudden flash of malice*) Yes! He's clever all right! (*Smiling again.*) You watch him answer, get round them with these notes, these papers of his. Think of the years he's been working on them—nearly five years. There must . . . there must be something really important in them. A great thick pile of papers . . . he treats them as if they were his very life. I can just see him reading out of them, proving things, making Dr. Bragg look small before the committee and the coroner. (*Sudden malignancy*) Oh, if only he didn't have them!

GLADYS (*echoing*)

Didn't have them?

MATRON (*another little laugh*)

Silly . . . wasn't it? But there! A person can't help their thoughts. And many a time as I went past that laboratory of his—with his papers all in there, (*intense voice*) many a time—I've thought, wouldn't it be a proper judgment . . . if . . .

GLADYS (*faintly*)

If what?

138

Don't you remember what we talked about! (*With a rush*) If they were to be destroyed, burned, finished with—again!

GLADYS (*staring at Matron*)

What are you saying?

MATRON

Nothing . . . nothing. I don't wish him no harm—in spite of all the cruel things he's said to me. (*Not looking at Gladys.*) After all, he's never done anything to me. But if he had (*low voice*), ah, now, there would be a way to hurt him, the only way. It's the only thing he cares about, (*quicker*) his work—it's his life blood, his soul, if he has one, the only thing he lives for—and it's all written down, calculations and figures and everything, on these paper sheets . . . in that little room there. (*Sudden change of tone*) My goodness! How I do run on! It's nearly time I was going over to the hall! Which reminds me. I mayn't have the opportunity to catch Dr. Bragg tonight. Would you be so kind as to give this to him. It's Dr. Venner's key. Dr. Bragg will want it first thing in the morning, for the committee. (*She offers the key to Gladys.*)

GLADYS (*recoils*)

No. (*Suddenly*) Yes, give it to me. (*She takes the key.*)

MATRON

Why, what's the matter, Mrs. Bragg?

GLADYS (*sits down rigidly*)

I . . . I have a headache.

MATRON

Dear, dear, I am so sorry.   You must rest a minute.
  GLADYS *turns directly facing door of laboratory R.*
Can I get you anything?

GLADYS

No, no.

MATRON

Well, I must see to Jennie.   (*Presses bell at mantelpiece.*)
  JENNIE *immediately* ENTERS *L., very spruce in clean apron
and cap.*
  Oh, Jennie, are you all finished up now?

JENNIE

Yes, Matron.

  The sound of dance music is heard in the distance.

MATRON

You'll not be wanted any more tonight.   You can go
over to the hall, straight away . . . for the dance.

140

JENNIE (*joyfully*)

Thank you, Matron.

JENNIE *goes towards door R.*

MATRON (*intercepting her*)

You can go this way for once.

JENNIE

Yes, Matron.

EXIT JENNIE *quickly Back Centre. As door opens dance music is heard more loudly, then fades.*

MATRON

Silly child! All for pleasure, these girls, nowadays. Well, I must follow her. (*Pauses.*) Will you come with me, Mrs. Bragg? (*Solicitously*) Or will you rest a minute in the quiet here with your headache?

GLADYS (*in a strangled voice*)

I'll—I'll rest a moment.

MATRON (*in a strange voice*)

I'll put this glare out for you. I'm always complaining about these top lights. They're very trying.

MATRON *switches out the top lights, leaving only the subdued standard lamp Back Centre. She stands, a silent, inscrutable figure, watching Gladys, then draws her cape about her shoulders. She turns,* EXIT *Back Centre.*

The dance music faintly continues.

141

GLADYS *remains seated as though stricken, then with a sudden hysterical determination she rises, moves to the door R., unlocks it, and flings it open. Wildly agitated, she gazes into the laboratory, then, turning swiftly, she picks up box of matches from mantelpiece and goes into the laboratory.*

While she is there MARY ENTERS *L. in a simple white frock. Unaware that Gladys is in the laboratory,* MARY *sees Venner's old lab. coat lying untidily on a chair. She smiles faintly, lifts it, hangs it up with a strange tenderness. At that moment* GLADYS *returns, door not quite closing behind her.*

MARY (*abruptly*)

Mrs. Bragg!

GLADYS (*hysterically*)

It's you! I'm glad—I'm glad it's you!

MARY (*urgent voice*)

What were you doing in there?

GLADYS (*weakly*)

I've just—I've just . . .

MARY *pushes past Gladys and runs into the laboratory. At the same instant* VENNER ENTERS *Back Centre.*

VENNER

Who—my God! (*He starts forward.*) Mary! (*shouting*) For God's sake watch out for that ether!

He rushes into the laboratory. At that instant there is a contained yet violent detonation which sends out a blinding flash of light. Dead silence follows.

(*From the laboratory*) Mary! Oh, my God! Mary!

Screaming, GLADYS RUNS OUT *of the room.*

CURTAIN

ACT III

SCENE: *The Same.*

TIME: *Thursday morning a month later.*

*The room is bright, the windows wide, admitting a sultry
sunshine.*

> JENNIE, *a black band on the arm of her red-and-white-
> striped uniform, is finishing dusting the alcove at rear.
> As she dusts she glances, from time to time, at* CHIVERS,
> *who paces impatiently, hat on the back of his head.*

CHIVERS

Look here, my girl! Sure you don't know where he is?

JENNIE

No, I told you, Mr. Chivers.

CHIVERS

All right, no offence. I can't help being a bit worked
up. What's the good me tearing over here on an empty
stomach if I can't get hold of him?

JENNIE

He should be in any minute.

144

You said that quarter an hour ago.   (*Pauses at door R.*)
  ENTER DREWETT *L., black tie.*

DREWETT

Has the mail come, Jennie?

JENNIE

No, sir.   (*Looking out window*) Oh, there's the postman
ust turning up the drive.

DREWETT

Run out and see what he has, will you?

JENNIE

Yes, sir.
  EXIT JENNIE *Back Centre.*

CHIVERS

Good morning, doctor!

DREWETT (*shortly*)

Morning.

CHIVERS

Painful tragedy you had here, sir, since I last had
he pleasure of seeing you. She was killed instantly, I
understand?

DREWETT (*moving away and taking up his white coat*)

Yes.

K   145

CHIVERS

'Streuth! She was pretty, too. I never rightly heard how she came to be in there?

DREWETT (*stiffly*)

We don't know, Mr. Chivers. But when the papers caught fire, she took a rug to beat them out. And she did beat them out, only an unimportant part of the manuscript was damaged. (*Pause.*) But she knocked over some ether—which ignited—and exploded a flask of tri-toluol.

CHIVERS

Dear, oh, dear! I understand Dr. Venner had a shocking burn, besides losing two fingers of his hand?

DREWETT, *changing into his white coat, turns his back, and does not answer.*

It didn't ought to have happened. Venner's a fellow should be left alone to get on with it in peace. (*Impatiently*) Can't you even think where he's likely to be, doctor?

DREWETT (*over shoulder*)

He sometimes takes a walk in West Avenue when his dressing's been done.

CHIVERS

West Avenue! I'll have a try! I can't stay put any longer!

He starts for door Back Centre, meets JENNIE *coming in, stops her confidentially.*

If any other gentleman, say the Mamley's representative, comes asking for Dr. Venner, you might have the presence of mind (*he presses a shilling upon her*) to say you don't know where he is.

JENNIE

But I don't, sir.

EXIT CHIVERS *Back Centre*.

DREWETT

Well!

JENNIE

Only the 'Journal', sir.

DREWETT *takes the 'Journal' from her and begins eagerly to tear off wrapper*.

ENTER MATRON *L*.

MATRON

Aren't you done here yet?

JENNIE

Just finishing, Matron.

DREWETT (*opening 'Journal'*)

Ah!

MATRON

You seem very interested, Dr. Drewett.

DREWETT

Do I?

MATRON

Anything fresh?

DREWETT

Yes.

EXIT DREWETT *Back Centre, reading ' Journal'.* JENNIE
drops her brush.

MATRON

Clumsy girl! Have you done your brasses?

JENNIE

Yes, Matron.

MATRON

Then tell Cook to parcel up these rotten oranges
complained about. Look sharp. The car's going in to
Parchester at twelve.

JENNIE

Very good, Matron.

EXIT JENNIE *R.*

ENTER THOROGOOD *Back Centre, quickly, dark suit and
black tie, an open ' Journal' in his hand.*

THOROGOOD

I say, where's the Chief?

MATRON

I haven't seen him since ten o'clock round.

THOROGOOD

They told me he was here. Good Lord! What's happened to everyone this morning? The place is at sixes and sevens.

MATRON

Can I help?

THOROGOOD

No, no, I can't wait. I must find him. It's important.
EXIT THOROGOOD *Back Centre.*
MATRON, *alone, goes slowly to the door R. She opens it, admitting a shaft of sunlight which reveals her expression as satisfied, fulfilled. At that moment* VENNER *slowly* ENTERS *L. His entry is strangely dramatic. He carries his left arm in a sling, his left hand is bandaged. He is pale and drawn from illness, his expression, though ironic and undefeated, is calmer than before.* MATRON *turns.*

VENNER

Well! Inspecting your new quarters, Matron?

MATRON

What if I was?

VENNER

It's a snug little place. When do the builders start work?

MATRON

Tomorrow.

VENNER *drifts to the piano, sits down on the piano stool and plays idly with his right hand.*

VENNER

I ought to take up the piano seriously. Everyone who used to loathe my playing will now say, " Poor fellow! Doesn't he do it marvellously with one hand? "

MATRON (*rigidly*)

You don't seem to mind?

VENNER (*gentle irony*)

What do you think? They say a little healthy mutilation is good for the soul—practised by all the best mystics. Who knows—in a few years' time I may be arranging myself on tenpenny nails.

MATRON

You still like your joke.

VENNER (*stops playing, faces her*)

It's been quite amusing lately. Watching you struggle with your baleful secret and Gladys dramatising her suburban remorse.

MATRON

Have you no feelings? You might at least make some show of being sorry she was killed.

VENNER (*suddenly, fiercely*)

Be quiet! For all your sickly mourning and moping none of you really give a damn whether she's alive or dead!

MATRON

And of course you do?

VENNER (*shouting*)

Leave my feelings out of it! Oh, blast! Why do I let you annoy me? (*Puts cigarette in mouth, fumbles with matchbox.*) Would you? I haven't got the knack of it yet.

MATRON *gazes at him stonily, then complies. When she goes to turn away, he detains her.*

As another of Britain's crippled heroes remarked— it was a glorious victory, wasn't it, Fanny?

MATRON

I don't know what you mean.

VENNER

That's one thing I admire about you. You're still heroically unreformed. Wasn't it Montaigne who said: " There are heroes in evil as well as good "? If you'd suddenly produced a better nature I'd have blown the gaff on you in sheer disgust.

ENTER BRAGG *Back Centre, a blue print in his hand.*

BRAGG

Morning, Matron. This should interest you. I've just passed them. The plans of your new sitting-room.

MATRON

Oh—Dr. Bragg.

BRAGG

Women don't understand these things—but look—this is the new french window.

MATRON

Yes, Dr. Bragg.

BRAGG

It should give you lots of sun. Well—there you are.

MATRON (*eyes downcast, biting her lips*)

I'm sure I appreciate your action from the bottom of my heart. It's been so awkward—all these years—difficult—for my position.

BRAGG (*rolling up print*)

Well, Venner! (*Forced affability*) How is the hand?

VENNER

Practically healed.

BRAGG (*heartily*)

I'm glad! For—ahem!—I'm afraid—(*Pause.*) Venner, I flatter myself I've behaved with commendable restraint. That the greatest day of my life—to date—should have been marred by such a catastrophe! But I never hit a man when he's down, I've said nothing these few weeks while you've loafed around. However, now . . .

VENNER

Justice must take its course?

BRAGG

Precisely. The postponed committee meeting is to-morrow forenoon. And in the afternoon, as chief magistrate, I must ask you to attend at Parchester.

VENNER

Well, well!

BRAGG

Naturally I wish—no scandal over Dr. Murray's passing!

VENNER

That's thoughtful of you.

BRAGG

But the failure of your research and Foster's death are immensely aggravated thereby. You must expect no leniency.

VENNER

You're making me nervous!

153

BRAGG (*rising indignation*)

Today at one o'clock I am interviewing two candidates, both well qualified, one a tennis blue, the other a most talented performer on the flute. Do I make myself clear?

VENNER

Perfectly.

BRAGG

You're very offhand, sir.

VENNER

Would you rather I burst a blood-vessel?

BRAGG (*greater indignation*)

I must say, in all my experience I have never met anyone so callous as yourself.

ENTER THOROGOOD *Back Centre, ' Journal ' in hand.*

THOROGOOD (*urgently*)

Oh, Chief! You're there!

BRAGG

Really, Dr. Thorogood . . .

THOROGOOD

I'm sorry, sir. But have you seen this?

BRAGG

Seen what?

THOROGOOD

Today's 'Medical Journal'.   (*Holding it out.*)

VENNER *detaches himself from group, strolls to piano and sits down.*

BRAGG

Upon my word, Thorogood!   (*Taking the ' Journal.'*) You know I'm far too busy to dawdle over even the ' Journal ' after breakfast.   (*Peevishly patting his vest pockets*) And I've left my glasses on my desk.   What is it?

THOROGOOD (*getting it out somehow*)

It's—it's Venner's thesis, sir.

VENNER *strikes soft chord on piano.*

THOROGOOD

Twenty pages—nearly half the ' Journal '—given over to it.   A special foreword from Sir George Gadsby, declaring it the biggest advance since Charcot.

Another chord from VENNER.

BRAGG

What do you mean?   Twenty pages?   Here?

THOROGOOD (*heavily but determinedly*)

Yes, sir.   There's no getting away from it.   Venner has proved his case—up to the hilt—it's we who were—who were in error.

BRAGG

Good heavens!

THOROGOOD

The microphotographs alone—the sections he took from Foster—they demonstrate unquestionable evidence of nerve-cell regeneration following his injections. I must play the game, Chief—and I will say they're brilliant—they're conclusive.

Bass chord from VENNER.

BRAGG

Then we—you were wrong about Foster.

THOROGOOD

Yes. But it isn't only that. This treatment of Venner's—oh, Lord! It takes a bit of admitting, sir . . . but it's going to mean an awful lot.

MATRON (*suddenly*)

I don't believe it!

Treble chord from VENNER.

THOROGOOD (*pointing to the ' Journal ' over Bragg's arm*)

See what Sir George says. "Nothing so momentous" —where is it?—look—" as this brilliantly sustained research from Hopewell Towers "!

156

BRAGG

Hopewell Towers!

Soft arpeggio from VENNER.

MATRON (*thrusting forward*)

Let me see! I can't, I won't believe it! (*She snatches the ' Journal ' from Bragg.*)

BRAGG (*slowly*)

Well, really, Dr. Venner—it would seem that, ahem! that we—we must congratulate you.

VENNER (*half-apologetically*)

A mean trick, wasn't it, to spring it on you like this?

BRAGG (*conflicting emotions*)

Far from it, my dear fellow. A pleasant, most pleasant surprise.

VENNER

They've suppressed half of the relevant equations. What's the odds? Not six people in the country would have understood them.

BRAGG (*unctuous smile*)

Sir George Gadsby has been convinced?

VENNER

Gadsby! He hasn't got the faintest notion what it's all about.

157

Bragg

Of course, my dear Venner, naturally this alters the whole position. All our little differences can easily be smoothed out, there's no question of your going now. We shall expect you to remain to work for the honour and glory of Hopewell Towers. Your laboratory . . .

Matron (*suddenly*)

Don't say it—don't!

Bragg

Matron!

Matron

You gave me that room, Dr. Bragg, you just showed me the plans.

Bragg

Nothing is begun yet.

Matron

But, Dr. Bragg! You promised! You don't know what it means to me!

Bragg

If Dr. Venner's work is important to this establishment and—and to humanity—he most assuredly must have it.

Matron (*rigid, imploring*)

You gave me that room. You—you couldn't take it back. I've wanted it for years. I've worked for it, put up with everything . . . and now it's mine—mine. I must have that room. . . .

BRAGG

Must!—Matron!

MATRON (*tortured voice*)

Can't you forget for once that I'm the Matron and remember I'm a woman. Haven't I served you, slaved for you? And why? Why? Can't you see how I've felt towards you—all these years!

BRAGG

Are you out of your senses?

MATRON (*intense trembling voice*)

Edgar! Please! Don't make me give it up—to him. If you only knew—I'll tell you. Hate me for it if you like. I'll tell you! He made love to your wife—your Gladys—behind the chapel—he made love to her—love . . .

She collapses into the chair, shaking, speechless.

THOROGOOD *and* VENNER *go to her assistance.*

VENNER

Loosen her collar.

THOROGOOD (*doing so*)

Good Lord! We'd better take her out.

159

BRAGG (*agitated*)

Yes, yes. Take her to her bedroom. Let her lie down
—with some weak tea—and—and thirty grains of bromide.

MATRON (*making a great effort*)

I'm all right. (*She rises, faces them.*) I'm sorry. I—
I overstepped my duty. I apologise—Dr. Bragg. (*She
goes towards door, erect but so slowly that* THOROGOOD *takes
her arm.*)

EXEUNT THOROGOOD *with* MATRON *L.*

BRAGG

Dear me! That was most painful! Never since I've
known her . . .

VENNER

We're all liable to go off half-cocked sometimes.

BRAGG (*darting a glance at Venner*)

But such things—she said. Really!

VENNER (*sombrely*)

She was hysterical.

BRAGG

They were so—so ridiculous—weren't they?

VENNER

We've all seen her devotion to you.

BRAGG

It isn't that—it's . . . (*forced laugh*) . . . well—
(*another glance at Venner*) Gladys . . .

VENNER

Don't you trust your wife, Dr. Bragg?

BRAGG

Indeed I do.

VENNER

Is there anything more to be said?

BRAGG (*without conviction*)

Of course not. I'll—I'll put the whole thing out of
my mind. I've no wish to jeopardise our most happily
restored relationship. Still—behind the chapel—what an
extraordinary idea!

ENTER CHIVERS *abruptly, Back Centre. He is heated.*

CHIVERS

Good morning, gentlemen. (*Mops his brow.*) I've
been chasing you all over the institution, Dr. Venner.

VENNER (*reproving*)

Mr. Chivers!

CHIVERS (*laughing heartily*)

Ha! Ha! Pretty good! I'm not one of that kind,
doctor. Whew! It's hot! Matter of fact, saving your

esteemed presence, Dr. Bragg, I was desirous of a couple of minutes' confab with you, Dr. Venner.

VENNER *pulls a packet of cigarettes from his pocket.* CHIVERS *immediately flashes a gold cigarette case at him.*

Allow me, sir.

VENNER

Thanks.   I prefer my own.

CHIVERS

Dr. Bragg? No? May I take the liberty? (*He selects and moistens a cigarette, flourishing an elaborate lighter.*) Always think they taste better out of a nice case.   Eighteen carat. (*Holds it up, weighs it.*)   Heavy.   Wish I could say it was a present from a grateful patient. Regret of my life—I'm always telling the missis. Mind you—I mix with them so much—I'm often taken for a professional gentleman.

BRAGG (*restively*)

Really, Mr. Chivers . . .

CHIVERS

Righto, Dr. Bragg. The fact is, I've a proposition for Dr. Venner from my firm—the handsomest proposition it's ever been my privilege to make. (*Scatters ash from cigarette.*)   Dr. Venner, you've been handicapped here—no offence, Dr. Bragg, needs must even in the finest private clinic—through working alone, insufficient equipment, inadequate safeguards—as witness your recent regrettable accident . . .

VENNER

We'll leave that out, Mr. Chivers.

CHIVERS

Certainly, certainly. I'll come straight to the point. (*Impressive and confidential*) Doctor! You know I been after you to pursue your work backed by the full resources of Glyster's! Think of it, doctor, our wonderful laboratory! White tiles everywhere! Electricity! Freshly laundered towels and lab. coats delivered every morning. Two thousand guinea-pigs to experiment with. A smart trained stenographer. . . .

VENNER (*sombrely*)

To experiment with?

CHIVERS (*unstoppable*)

Racks of test-tubes. Instruments of precision. Our centrifuge alone, steam driven, the largest of its kind in Europe!

VENNER

You've no oyster bar!

CHIVERS (*pained*)

We have a modern, hygienic cafeteria in the basement. Doctor! I won't beat about the bush! I'll give you the good news outright. We offer you the post—not assistant —but chief research physician at the Glyster Laboratories.

Ah!—of course—you'd want me to bring my formula along?

Why, naturally, doctor; that's part and parcel of our plan to help you. There's no house in the world can handle it like Glyster's—go-ahead yet safe—conservative yet liberal. For God's sake don't give it to Mamley's—they'd hawk it round like chewing-gum. *And* we're ethical. We'll take care of all your professional scruples.

CHIVERS (*quiet scorn*)

What's your idea? Put up a weak solution? It would go well as a nerve tonic!

CHIVERS (*enthusiastically*)

Now you're talking, doctor! You begin to see the possibilities! I'd a great idea coming over. The name—everything's in a name as Shakespeare said—it's important. Nervsan. Nerv—nerves; san—health. Pretty good, eh?

VENNER *begins quietly and bitterly to laugh.*

VENNER

And how much do I get for all this?

CHIVERS

Your salary, doctor—the handsome figure of £1,000.

BRAGG (*impressed*)

£1,000!

CHIVERS

Per annum. Our Mr. Glyster's no stinter; he wired me this morning to go and get you.

VENNER

Then wire him back you've failed.

CHIVERS

Ah! I understand your hesitation, Dr. Venner. I should have been a doc. myself. Besides, this is your big moment—you just had your little article accepted by the 'Journal'—human nature being what it is, I don't blame you if you want to cash in. Now I'll put all my cards on the table. There's probably nothing in your stuff. But money doesn't matter to the House of Glyster. Commercially speaking apart, we find it helps our reputation to foster original research. Therefore, doctor, on behalf of my house, I increase my offer to £1,100. And take it or leave it, that's my final word.

VENNER

Nothing doing.

CHIVERS

£1,200. And a five years' engagement.

VENNER

You mean sentence.

BRAGG

Dr. Venner has a sense of loyalty to the institution

which sponsored and encouraged his work. I'm sure, despite your generous terms, he'll prefer to remain with us.

CHIVERS

£1,500, and that's my limit.

VENNER (suddenly tired of it)

Oh! go to hell!

CHIVERS (mopping his brow)

You're a hard man to deal with, Venner. And, by God! you're no fool, either. I felt it in my bones you'd want a bonus. Listen!—on the qt.! Mr. Glyster is coming down here personally. In fact, he's on his way now. Give me time to contact him before you fix with Mamley's?

VENNER

I shan't fix with anyone.

CHIVERS

It's a bargain. (<i>Looks quickly at his watch</i>) I've just time to meet the express at Parchester. Hold everything, doctor, till I bring the boss. This is big, for me and you. <i>Au revoir</i>, gentlemen, till we meet again.

EXIT CHIVERS, <i>Back Centre</i>.

BRAGG

Shall you accept his offer?

166

VENNER

What offer? The one he's made or the one he's going to make?

BRAGG

Naturally—the money is a great inducement. Why, even my own income—(*hastily*) of course, I have my house.

VENNER

I daresay I could shake down in the centrifuge.

BRAGG

My dear Venner—we must bury the hatchet once and for all. At the committee meeting tomorrow—I promise you full vindication—we'll induce you to stay with us at all costs.

VENNER

What about these police proceedings?

BRAGG

My dear fellow! Wiped out, instantly! As senior J.P., I assure you! All that stupid woman Foster's doing—I never heard such nonsense in my life.

ENTER GLADYS, *Back Centre. She is dressed in black. Her expression is set, curiously dull, her tone almost expressionless.*

GLADYS

Edgar! Three reporters have arrived—asking about betrazol!

BRAGG

Reporters!

GLADYS

One from the " Parchester Herald ", two from London papers.   They're waiting in your study.

BRAGG (*excited*)

This is most gratifying. You must let me deal with them, Venner.

GLADYS

And another car passed me as I came across the drive.

BRAGG

I'll get over at once. Let me think. I shall want the new photographs, Gladys, especially the views of the dairy farm. Ask Dr. Thorogood to fetch them—File P from the office—also you might send in some refreshments presently—not the best sherry.

He goes to the door, recollects suddenly, glances from one to the other.

You won't be too long, dear?

GLADYS

No, Edgar.

BRAGG

I'd like a word with you—Gladys—later.

GLADYS

A word with me?

BRAGG (*half deprecating, half suspicious*)

Yes, about—about the—the garden, my dear. I was thinking of having the shrubbery cut down—behind the chapel.

GLADYS (*suddenly rigid*)

Were you? Why?

BRAGG

Well—just an idea—my love!

GLADYS (*like ice*)

Is there anything behind this—brilliant suggestion?

BRAGG (*returning hastily*)

No, no, my dear. Why! I know you're—well—of course——

He puts his hand on her arm and propitiatingly, possessively, strokes it. She bears with the caress, then cannot, any longer.

GLADYS (*strangled voice*)

Please . . . don't, Edgar.

BRAGG (*fondly*)

My pet!

GLADYS (*low voice, all her veiled antipathy released*)

Take your hands away!

BRAGG

Yes, yes, my dear. (*To Venner apologetically*) Everything's been a great shock to her. (*Moving to door*) It's worried her terribly—to see me upset!

EXIT BRAGG *Back Centre.*

GLADYS (*puts hand to head, collects herself and says quietly*)
What do these reporters want?

VENNER

What does any reporter want? The headlines tomorrow will read: "New Hope for the Afflicted. Brilliant Discovery Wins £20,000-Year Job for Struggling Researchist." Or even, with luck: "Heroic Woman Gives Life for Science." Below will be two columns chiefly—if I know your husband—advertising Hopewell Towers.

GLADYS (*unhappily*)
Paul, I'm disappointed in you.

VENNER

I'm most damnably disappointed in myself.

GLADYS

Are they really going to give you all that money?

VENNER

More—if I drive a hard bargain. (*He laughs.*)

GLADYS

What is there to laugh at?

VENNER

It's funny—the idea of me peddling out my shop-soiled soul, well diluted, for the benefit of the Glyster stockholders.

GLADYS

Why can't you enjoy your success? (*Gazing pleadingly at him*) Oh, Paul! Isn't there just one word—that you could say to me!

VENNER (*old cynicism*)

Nothing you'd particularly care to hear.

GLADYS (*low voice*)

Can't you even give me credit—for having suffered? (*Genuine feeling*) If you knew how I'd cried my eyes out every night . . .

VENNER

I've no doubt it's been a great spiritual experience for you!

GLADYS

Why are you so heartless—to me, to everyone! (*Low voice*) You—you never go to her grave, do you?

VENNER

Never.

GLADYS

Not a day passes but I send down flowers.

VENNER

What a mess it must be!

GLADYS

Then look at your tie.

VENNER (*squinting down*)

It's the only one I've got.

GLADYS

The colour! You might at least have done that for her. I shan't go out of mourning for six months.

VENNER

It isn't your fault that black suits you.

GLADYS (*passionately*)

For pity's sake!—You're as hard as stone! Will you never realise?—I didn't want to hurt her—I was jealous of course, but I—I was fond of her. It all happened—everything—because I loved you!

VENNER

I'm quite willing to take the blame.

GLADYS

Oh, God! What am I to say? What am I to do?

172

Paul! Is it too late? Couldn't we—begin all over again—together!

VENNER

Walk hand in hand—into the rosy sunset?

GLADYS

We've been through so much. We could help each other. I'd make up for all I've done. I know I'm selfish and vain. I'd try to be better. . . .

VENNER (*bitter laugh*)

Next thing you'll be giving away Edgar's old clothes to the Parchester relief—entering a convent—or proposing to have a leetle che-ild! Unless, of course, next month sees you taking tennis lessons—or some gentle instruction on the flute!

GLADYS (*sincere angry outburst*)

You cruel, heartless beast!—I wish you'd been killed instead of her!

VENNER (*turning towards her, suddenly serious*)

Gladys! I like you for that—more than I have done— ever! (*Pause.*) I know you're sincere in feeling upset. (*Pause.*) Unfortunately it upsets me to feel sincere!

GLADYS

Well! (*Bitter sigh.*) I suppose it is all over between us. And what an ending! But at least I have the

173

satisfaction—I saved you for your work—kept you from burying yourself in the wilds of China.

VENNER (*return to irony*)

Posterity will thank you!

ENTER THOROGOOD *L.*

THOROGOOD

She's quieter now. But I did have a job. Thought I should have had to send for one of the male attendants.

VENNER

Probably more effective than the tea.

GLADYS (*moving to go out*)

Dr. Bragg wants you to fetch File P from the office.

THOROGOOD

Just a minute, Mrs. Bragg. (*Awkwardly*) Look here, Venner.

VENNER

Oh, my God!

THOROGOOD

It's a ruddy hard thing for a chap to do. But I—I want to apologise.

VENNER

Must you?

THOROGOOD

Yes, honestly! You were right and I was wrong. You've handed me an awful facer. But I'll do my level best to play up. . . .

VENNER (*trying to get away*)

Fine.

THOROGOOD

And I'm jolly sorry I threatened to sock you on the jaw. I hope we'll pull together in the future. . . .

VENNER (*another effort to escape*)

Not another cross word shall pass between us!

THOROGOOD

No, don't go, Venner. I'm not a bloke that says much, but believe me I've sympathised with you in your loss. You know I've got the sweetest girl in the world myself. If anything happened to—to separate us, I'd go crackers.

VENNER

Would you really?

THOROGOOD

Phyllis is so dependable, I feel she's always there, absolutely normal. It's none of my business, of course, but it seems to me, Venner, scientifically speaking, that poor Mary had an Oedipus complex!

VENNER (*stiffens suddenly*)

Will you shut up?

THOROGOOD

But don't you see—her fixation in God, her father and his missionary work—nothing could have broken it.

VENNER (*furiously*)

You fool!

VENNER *knocks Thorogood down.*

GLADYS

Oh, Paul—what have you done!

VENNER

I've meant to do it for months.

GLADYS

George! Are you hurt?

THOROGOOD

Yes, no. (*Getting up slowly*) Of course I can't hit you when you're disabled.

VENNER

More fool you! You'll never have a better chance.

GLADYS

Leave him, George.

176

THOROGOOD

We'll have this out later, Venner. (*Holding his jaw.*) I'm ready if you are, Mrs. Bragg. I'm sure the Chief's waiting on you.

GLADYS (*a mortal resignation in her voice*)

Yes . . . he's waiting . . . on me.

EXEUNT THOROGOOD *and* GLADYS. ENTER JENNIE *L.*

JENNIE

Mr. Chivers on the 'phone, sir.

VENNER

Tell him I'm engaged.

JENNIE

Very good, sir.

VENNER

Oh, Jennie! There's a suitcase in my room. Would you shove my things in it for me?

JENNIE (*astonished*)

D'you mean—pack, sir?

VENNER *nods. Pause.*

Yes, sir.

EXIT JENNIE *L.* VENNER *moves slowly to the mantel-piece, picks up the small framed photograph of Mary and gazes at it fixedly. Sound of the door causes him hurriedly to shove*

M 177

*it in the pocket of his lab. coat, hanging near. He remains
rigid at mantelpiece. DREWETT ENTERS. The old man has,
for once, lost his detachment.*

DREWETT

Well, Venner! You've rung the bell this time!

VENNER

Have I?

DREWETT

The place is simply humming. It's all through the
wards. Sister Hall is smashing feeding-cups with ex-
citement.

VENNER

Is she?

DREWETT

When you go over you'll run into something like a
civic reception.

VENNER

Shall I?

DREWETT

I'd have given something to have seen Bragg's face.

VENNER (*with an effort*)

It's still on view.

178

DREWETT (*chuckling.   Hands a bunch of telegrams*)

These have just come for you.   Congratulations from
every hypocrite in Harley Street.   It means nothing to
me, of course, Venner.   But I always swore you were
less of a clown than you looked!

VENNER

I couldn't be more of one than I feel!   (*Pockets the
telegrams unopened.*)   With the best intentions in the world
I've just sent Matron into a fit, insulted Mrs. Bragg and
knocked Thorogood down.

DREWETT

Well, I've been through the 'Journal' twice.   Forgive
me if I say I don't understand a word of it!

VENNER (*slowly*)

I wonder now how I did it.   (*The telephone rings outside.*)
You know, Drewett, it's like painting a picture, like
composing a symphony, a matter of moods and surges of
emotion—impossible to recapture them.   I'd never have
written it again.

ENTER JENNIE *L.*

JENNIE

Mr. Chivers said if you were engaged, sir, would I
give you a message.   Would you lunch with him and
Mr. Glyster without fail at the Lion Hotel, Parchester,
at one o'clock?

VENNER

Tell him Dr. Venner—regrets—he's unable to lunch today.

JENNIE

Very well, sir.

EXIT JENNIE *L.*

DREWETT

Don't you like champagne?

VENNER

Not when it goes with brown boots and back-slapping.

DREWETT

I remember when these people adopted Dr. Pflagg— the half-starved little Austrian who discovered mesonyl. The last I heard of him he was buying Renoirs.

VENNER

Renoir's women are too fat for me.

ENTER JENNIE *L.*

JENNIE

Mr. Chivers is leaving by car with Mr. Glyster immediately. They'll be here by 1.15—without fail.

VENNER *nods.* EXIT JENNIE *L.*

DREWETT

Manet's women were nicer.

VENNER

Too nice.

The telephone rings very loud.

DREWETT

They mean you to have an art collection at all costs.

JENNIE ENTERS *L.*

JENNIE

That was Mamley's, sir. A trunk call from London. I said I thought you wasn't available.

VENNER

Quite right.

JENNIE

And Dr. Bragg has just been on the house 'phone, sir. He has four gentlemen of the press waiting to see you. He wants to know when he may expect you over for a cocktail.

DREWETT

Aha! Not the cheap sherry!

VENNER

Oh, say (*pause*), say I'm on the point of leaving. And, Jennie?

JENNIE

Yes, sir?

VENNER

Did you pack my case?

JENNIE

Just finishing, sir.

VENNER

Then bring it down, like a good girl. And my rain-coat.

JENNIE

Certainly, sir.

EXIT JENNIE *L.* *The sky has darkened outside.*

DREWETT

You taking a week-end off to dodge them? Good idea.

VENNER

A longish week-end, Drewett.

DREWETT

You'll have dirty weather, I'm afraid. Storm's coming up. Where are you going?

VENNER

China.

DREWETT

Where? (*Pauses, greatly upset.*) Oh, no! You don't mean that!

182

VENNER (*faint smile*)

I've always wanted to taste the real birds'-nest soup.

DREWETT (*loudly*)

Good heavens alive, man! Will you drop that infernal flippancy? You're not going out there?

VENNER

I assure you, Drewett, seriously, that I am going. At twelve o'clock the car leaves here with a parcel of decayed oranges. I shall accompany them—appropriately—as far as Parchester. I reach Liverpool tonight. My boat sails tomorrow. It's all arranged. In four weeks I'll be in Shantchen.

DREWETT (*voice still raised*)

But why?

VENNER

Pure research!

DREWETT (*louder*)

Pure tomfoolery!

VENNER

Don't fracture my eardrum. It's true. I want to try out betrazol in cerebro-spinal fever. They've got it there—a really virulent epidemic in a nice tropical setting. Just my line.

DREWETT

You're a rotten liar!

VENNER

Well—I'm rotten all through.

DREWETT

What in the name of heaven's happened to you?

VENNER

I don't know! (*Under great stress*) I'm knocked out! I can't tell where I stand! But I can't believe any more that it all ends in dust, Drewett! I must believe in something—that I used to think—impossible!

DREWETT (*quietly*)

So that's it!

VENNER (*rigid*)

Good of you not to laugh!

DREWETT (*low voice*)

The joke will probably strike me later!

VENNER

How I would have jeered a month ago! A brand from the burning! I was too clever, Drewett; I satirised my own emotions once too often. (*With greater intensity*) When she lay in my arms in the lab. and looked up at me with her last flicker of life—oh, God!—I can't tell you what I felt. The agonised sensation of a million years. And through it all I felt how little I was and how rotten. I felt all my uselessness, my silly self-complacency, my cheap little love affairs. But most of all I felt—I felt that in her outlook, her conception of life, she was right and I was wrong.

DREWETT

So now you believe in her God?

VENNER

I wish to God I could! All that's happened for the moment—I've lost my own. But if there is a God— what fun he's had! Love and sacrifice—a joke in rather bad taste I called it. And then he played that very joke on me.

DREWETT (*sadly*)

Women!—they're such a damned nuisance! But you must have loved her very much.

VENNER

I did love her, Drewett. And, all the time, I feel she died for love of me. (*Quickly*) Don't you see why I can't settle? I must move. I'm driven by something within myself. I can't wait to see this place she was going to— the hospital, what they're doing there—this man King who

185

cables me like a machine-gun. I'll probably fight with him like hell. But still, I must go, I simply must!

DREWETT (heavily)

I think—I understand. (Pause.) Do you know, Venner—I'm too old to start worrying about the hereafter—and all these depressing problems of eternity which seem terrible at forty and nothing at all at seventy. What would you think of it, at my time of life, if I suddenly turned round—for instance—and asked you why we were here on earth below? (Pause.) But why the devil are we here? Is it for no other reason than to eat, sleep, and exploit our organs of reproduction? Most people seem to think so, and they get away with it. Or do they? For sometimes quite suddenly there comes a shattering experience—a thunderbolt, the writing on the wall, a burst of ironic laughter from the sky, perhaps less harrowing than your experience, perhaps more so. Pestilence, famine, war—not one death, but the deaths of thirteen million. And why—why—why? Man's stupidity, blind circumstance or retribution?—I don't think so! (Pause.) I'd rather say—a warning! Do you remember that sickly line in some maudlin, moribund song—" He Marks the Sparrow's Fall "?—awful, I know—but suppose someone were really marking the movements of us sparrows—watching our silly, greedy, selfish flutterings—and suddenly, once in a while, tweaking us back—painfully—from our exploits in the gutter. Oh! I daresay I'm talking rubbish. But suppose every catastrophe in life had a preordained purpose—was to be used for the spiritual advantage of the individual! I remember reading

186

a long time ago in some ridiculous essay that no soul was ever lost without being shown the signpost once—without having had a lesson in atonement. I wonder—Venner— if that was your lesson?

VENNER (*staring at him*)

My God! You make me wonder too!

ENTER JENNIE *R. with suitcase and raincoat.*

JENNIE

Shall I put them here, sir? (*Puts down suitcase and raincoat.*)

VENNER

Thank you, Jennie.

EXIT JENNIE *L.*

DREWETT (*gazing at the suitcase sadly*)

So soon as this? It's going to be quite a relief—not to see your ugly face at breakfast—any more.

VENNER

How you've put up with me I don't know!

DREWETT

Well—it was—occasionally—rather a painful struggle.

He begins to laugh, but the laugh suddenly breaks. He coughs and turns away.

187

VENNER

Of course—it must be a great disappointment for you —me interrupting my work.

DREWETT

Your work! (*Oddly*) Do you really imagine—now I'm nearing the worms—that I care twopence whether a million schizophrenics are restored to bounding health or choke themselves with mattress stuffing in a million padded rooms?

VENNER

But I thought . . .

DREWETT (*with quiet sincerity*)

Sentiment has got me into trouble even in my dotage. My marriage was not exactly a successful one. Indeed, my whole life's been a failure. Yet at the end of it—I had a lot of happiness—like a silly old maid—fancying I had a son.

A pause.

VENNER

I'll miss you too, Drewett. You'll let me hear from you?

DREWETT

I'll be as big a nuisance as Phyllis. (*Sighs.*)

VENNER

Cheer up, man. Think of the fun you'll have receiving my distinguished visitors.

DREWETT

What shall I tell them?

VENNER

Oh—say the matron has set me up in a row of houses in Bognor.

DREWETT

You'd find that healthier than Shantchen.

VENNER

Rot! Shantchen—to quote the Chinese Baedeker—is not without its attractions. They were bombed three times last week. Think of the reactions of the nervous system—especially the children. I'll send you a snapshot —Dr. Paul Venner on Chop-Stick, his favourite dromedary. (*He looks at his watch*) Must watch my time.

DREWETT

Is there anything I can do for you now?

VENNER

Only the car. I have a few odds and ends to collect here. I don't want it to miss me.

DREWETT

Well, I'll see about it for you. It's going to pour with rain any minute.

EXIT DREWETT *slowly Back Centre.*

ENTER JENNIE *L.*

That 'phone again, sir. It's . . .

VENNER *checks her.*

Good-bye, sir.

EXIT JENNIE *L.*

VENNER *stands alone in the room. He takes his suitcase, places it upon the table, opens it, collects his books from the alcove and flings them into the case. He comes upon his gramophone record, picks it up as though to smash it but, on an impulse, puts it on the gramophone. He listens, then takes Mary's photograph from his lab. coat and puts it quietly in the case, which he closes. Then, as he discards lab. coat, the Testament falls out of the pocket. There is a strange stillness in his figure. He picks it up, studies it, makes to fling it in the wastepaper basket, refrains, slowly puts it in his pocket. Quickly he takes hat and raincoat, picks up suitcase. The gramophone is still playing as he* EXITS.

CURTAIN

THE END